D1488180

London
for FREE

Sixth edition

© Harden's Limited, 2009

ISBN 978-1-873721-87-2

British Library Cataloguing-in-Publication data:
a catalogue record for this book is available from
the British Library.

Printed and bound in Finland by
WS Bookwell

Research Assistant: Rebecca Halfond
Prodution Assistant: Fiona Aranguren

Harden's Limited
14 Buckingham Street
London WC2N 6DF

Contents

Introduction

What can you do in London for free?

World-famous parks, beautiful ancient woodlands, great museums and galleries, spectacular annual events and superb entertainments – the capital has an unrivalled range of free attractions.

In fact, London is probably the very best major city in the world for things to do for free. Paris's Louvre and New York's Metropolitan Museum of Art may have great collections, for example, but you have to pay handsomely to see them. Not so at the British Museum or our National Gallery. (In fact, the Director of the British Museum recently declined the flattering offer from the Metropolitan Museum to poach him, explicitly on the basis that the fabulously rich NYC institution was not open to all the world.)

As you will see, whatever your age and interests, whether you're a parent with children to entertain, a Londoner wanting to explore or a visitor to this great city, you really can do a lot of wonderful things here without paying a penny.

Is everything in this book free?

Yes. Except where clearly stated to the contrary, all the suggested activities in this book are substantially free of charge. These aren't weasel words: what we mean is that you can enjoy a visit for free, even if there may also be some 'extra' you could pay for. We wouldn't, for example, decline to list a church because you have to pay to go up the bell tower. We also count as 'free' the many essentially free-access museums and galleries which sometimes charge entry fees for special exhibitions.

If an asterisk (*) appears next to a name, however, this means that free access is substantially restricted. The attraction may be free only at certain times (in which case the times we give in the small print are only those when there is no charge), or you may have access only to a relatively small part of the building.

Just in case there is any confusion, where shops, markets, pubs or cafés are mentioned, they are included because we thought it would be helpful for you to know about them or because they offer great window-shopping opportunities. We're not suggesting that the goods and services they offer are free of charge.

Introduction and organisation

And transport for free?

Sadly, transport – Shanks's pony aside – also must be paid for. We would recommend any visitor to buy a Transport for London Travelcard – they are very good value and once you have one you can zip around the capital with no regard to expense.

Daily Travelcards can be bought after 9.30am and, subject to zone restrictions, allow unlimited transport on buses, tubes, Docklands Light Railway and Tramlink trains.

Once you have a Travelcard, you can explore London from the best possible vantage point – the upper platform of a double-decker bus – at no cost. This form of tour has the virtue that you can hop on and hop off to your heart's content. If you find there are so many things to do you don't have time to finish your planned circuit, it hardly matters.

With one of Transport for London's free bus guides, you can plan your own tour, but there are two routes which are particularly suitable for a general orientation.

The number 11 takes you on a great East-West tour of London, and includes many of the major sights. Start your trip at a stop in Chelsea's fashionable King's Road and ride through Victoria to Westminster Abbey. This would be a good place to break the journey and to walk a short way – through Parliament Square, and down Whitehall to look at 10 Downing Street and the Cenotaph. Get back on the bus at Trafalgar Square – having admired Nelson's Column and, if time permits, visited the National Gallery. Travel down the Strand and Fleet Street, and end at St Paul's Cathedral.

The number 15 (pick it up at Paddington, Edgware Road, Oxford Street or Regent Street) shares the Trafalgar Square to St Paul's section with the number 11 (so you can change at any point between the two). However, the 15 continues on into the City enabling you to see the Monument, Tower Bridge and the Tower of London. Travel on this route on a Sunday morning and you might press on to Aldgate, for Petticoat Lane market.

For more information on getting the best out of your Travelcard, see "Public Transport" on page 14.

Organisation

How is the book laid out?

First, geographically. We've split London into six areas, starting with Central (which is mainly the area usually called the West End). The next three are West (starting at Hyde Park), North (starting at Regents Park) and South (including everything south of the river). Going eastwards, we've subdivided the world into The City (EC postcodes) and East London (E postcodes). Map references are given, where applicable, after the website and telephone number.

Secondly, as in England everything depends on the weather, we've divided each of the above sections into indoor and outdoor attractions. The introduction to each chapter summarises the highlights of the area concerned. In addition, we've suggested sightseeing walks in most areas, to help you get your bearings and to 'join up' the various free attractions in the vicinity.

We have given the most up-to-date information available, but details change and it's always a good idea to check websites to confirm opening times and any other details of particular interest before setting off. If you are making a special trip, you should always confirm the arrangements that apply over holiday periods – opening hours may be modified, of course, but there may also be special events worth knowing about.

Indexes

If you're interested in a particular type of attraction, wherever in town it is to be found, don't miss the indexes. There, we've given lists of all the museums, all the parks, all the galleries, and so on, to make sure you don't miss out on anything.

We hope that this book will help you to find London as fascinating a place as we continually do. And if you find something we've missed, please do write to tell us: the best way is to send an email to mail@hardens.com.

Richard Harden   **Peter Harden**

*Londonwide
information*

General information

The web
The web has transformed access to information about
what you can do in London for free, in particular when it
comes to event-related (time and date-sensitive)
information.

We assume for the purposes of this guide that you have
access to the web. If you do not, some libraries offer free
internet access (if sometimes only to registered
members). The most central such service is Westminster
Reference Library. Bookings are taken in advance and you
are limited to an hour's use at any one time.
Understandably it's very popular. Bookings:
(020) 7641 1300. (Times: Mon-Fri 10am-8pm, Sat
10am-5pm).

If you Google "London for free", you won't want for
listings websites. The best of them, it seems to us, is
www.freelondonlistings.co.uk – just run your cursor over
the 'calendar', and you're presented with a nice neat list of
free things to do on that particular day. Another site well
worth cheking out is www.londonisfree.com. Once you've
exhausted this book – it may take a while! – you'll find
these sites invaluable.

Libraries
If you're out and about in central London, it's very difficult
to find yourself far from a public library. You don't of
course need to be a resident of the area concerned to go
and browse through the newspapers, listings magazines
and guide books. They are an excellent source of
inspiration.

The most central comprehensive resources are to be
found at:

Westminster Reference Library, just by Leicester Square
35 St Martin's Street WC2, (020) 7641 1300

Victoria
160 Buckingham Palace Road SW1, (020) 764 1300

Chelsea
Old Town Hall, King's Road SW3, (020) 7361 3010

St Pancras
opposite the railway station NW1, (020) 7974 5833

Swiss Cottage
88 Avenue Road NW3, (020) 7974 6522

For details of libraries in your area, see your local council
website, or the telephone directory.

Most libraries will also have London titles both for reference and (for members) to borrow without charge. There are perhaps the best source of inspiration for the many many special interests which you can pursue in London without cost, upon which there is much more information than we are able to set out here. They should also have general travel guides to London. The most, comprehensive general guide is probably the *Eyewitness Travel Guide* (Dorling Kindersley, 2009), with listings, pictures and descriptions of galleries, museums, walks and architecture. Other guides of note include those published by Time Out, Rough Guides and Lonely Planet.

Free daily newspaper

Metro – the daily free morning newspaper – can be picked up at Underground stations each weekday – look for the blue metal dump bins. You'll need to be quick, as they're usually all gone by 9am. In addition to general news, it has listings of events happening that day, including free or inexpensive sources of entertainment.

From mid-afternoon onwards, you can pick up copies of London Lite *and* thelondonpaper *– free newspapers with lots of listing information – throughout central London.*

Ms London, Girl About Town, Nine to Five, Midweek, London Monthly…

An ever-changing range of magazines aimed at differing sections of London's inhabitants (South Africans, Canadians, South Americans…) are available from dump bins outside principal tube and rail stations. As well as articles, listings and reviews, they often include discount vouchers for services and even the occasional offer of a free haircut..

TNT

www.tntonline.co.uk

It may not be quite as comprehensive as Time Out *(which is free only on consultation in public libraries), but* TNT *– the weekly magazine for expat Aussies and Kiwis – is obtainable without any charge and has quite good theatre, cinema and other event listings. It also includes details of the many free slide shows organised by the main trekking and adventure companies to publicise their holidays. There are also articles of general budget interest, too. Pick a copy up from the publication's spiritual home – outside Earl's Court tube – or from street dispensers throughout central London, including major rail and tube stations.*

Tourist information centres

When it comes to things to do and see, tourist information offices can be just as much use to residents as to visitors. Sadly, their number has declined in recent years. We've listed the principal survivors in the relevant geographical sections of the guide. Details of the only central office are as follows:

Britain and London Visitor Centre (BLVC) SW1
www.visitlondon.com
1 Regent St   (0870) 156 6366   2–2C
Curiously – bizarrely, you might think – London does not currently have an official dedicated stand-alone tourist office. That's no disrespect to the Britain and London Visitor Centre, handily located not far from Piccadilly Circus, which offers the coverage its name suggests. Especially if you're new to London, it's well worth popping in, as you'll find lots of free information about things to do (both free and otherwise). And you might even get some tips for free things to do outside the capital (which are, of course, outside the scope of this book).
/ Times: Mon 9.30am–6.30pm, Tue–Fri 9am–6.30pm, Sun 10am–4pm (2 Jan–31 May: Sat 10am–4pm; 1 June-30 Sep: Sat 9am–5pm)
1 Oct – 30 Dec, Sat 10.00 – 16.00; www.visitlondon.com; Tube: Piccadilly Circus.

Getting about

Public transport
www.tfl.gov.uk
(020) 7222 1234
Transport for London runs the Underground, buses, the Docklands Light Railway, river services and Victoria Coach Station. As well as a 24-hour telephone service, it has an excellent website, which any resident (or longer-term visitor) will find it well worth becoming familiar with.

There is also a Travel Information Office on the concourse of Victoria Station (opposite platform 8), which is an excellent source of maps and brochures to enable you to use London's public transport efficiently. There are further offices at: Heathrow Terminals 1, 2 and 4; and at the Terminals 1, 2, and 3 Underground stations (Mon-Sat); West Croydon; Euston; Hammersmith (Mon-Sat); Piccadilly Circus; St James's Park (Mon-Fri); Liverpool Street; Oxford Circus; Paddington (Mon-Sun).

A series of free leaflets entitled Simply London – with information on various topics – is available from most Underground stations or from the website. / Times: Mon-Sat 7.15am-9.15pm; Sun & Bank Holidays 8.15am-8.15pm; Tube: Victoria.

Cycling

www.tfl.gov.uk

It's very much the Mayor policy to get people 'on their bikes'. For suggestions of bicycle routes, and much more about cycling in the metropolis, visit the Transport for London website.

Walking

www.walklondon.org.uk

www.tfl.gov.uk

Walking in London is not just a cheap way of getting from A to B, as it is perhaps when you're walking around the capital that Dr Johnson's cliché (the one about being tired of life) is most obviously true. The things that really make the city special are generally as obvious to a pauper as to a prince, and they're often better appreciated from a pavement than from a limousine.

There's a lot to be said for walking aimlessly. Certainly in central London, it's almost impossible not to stumble upon something of interest.. You can of course take a map with you, but some people think it spoils the fun.

If your tastes are more structured, though, the ever-useful www.tfl.gov.uk website again becomes relevant. The Walks section you can click to at the bottom of the homepage leads you through to six suggestions for walks around the capital.

These six walks not personal enough for you? The site's journey planner – accessible from the homepage (click 'Advanced options') – can be programmed to produce a walking itinerary just for you!. The trick is to increase the time you're prepared to walk, and the itineraries produced will then include a walk-only option. You can then even print off a custom map, which will show you all the major sites along the way.

If you're looking for something more in the nature of a country walk – for which London offers many possibilities – check out the www.walklondon.org.uk website. You can get information online, or they'll even send you leaflets without charge.

Skating

www.citiskate.com

For a free trip round the capital, why not just get your skates on? Most weeks see a marshalled Friday night skating tour of London. It's called the Friday Night Skate (and is "accompanied by a portable sound system" too). Meet at the Duke of Wellington Arch, Hyde Park Corner. The skate lasts from 8pm-10pm. Check out details on the website.

For a gentler bit of exercise, the Roller Stroll takes place every Sunday at 2pm. Gather at the east end of Serpentine Road (within Hyde Park, not far from the Queen Elizabeth Gate, the one that was erected in memory of the late Queen Mother).

Disabled access

*There are several services which are very helpful for disabled
people who are exploring London. For general information (and
useful links) the prime source is www.visitlondon.com.*

*Queries relating in any way to travel for the disabled and
elderly (and including information about hire of vehicles) can be
addressed to Transport for London (tel 020 7222 1234). As on
so many topics, there is a lot of relevant information on the
www.tfl.gov.uk website, from which you can dowload a guide
called* Getting Around London.

*To check out the details of the access arrangements for any
place of entertainment or tourist attraction in London you can
visit Artsline's website (www.artsline.org.uk). Artsline also
distributes a range of access guides, including some to tourist
attractions (nominal charge). Also worth consulting is
www.officiallondontheatre.co.uk/access, which holds details on
disabled access to the capital's theatres. For those interested in
finding physical activities, The organisation called Disability
Sports also has a useful website – www.disabilitysports.co.uk,
where one can find information on trampolining and swimming
groups, amongst others.*

Topic information

Architecture
www.londonarchitecturediary.com
*An informative website with full daily listings of all things
architectural going on in London, such as exhibitions, talks,
debates, tours and events, a lot of which are free.*

Art galleries and museums
www.24hourmuseum.org.uk
*This 'national virtual museum' is a state-funded website which
has the aim of promoting museums, galleries and heritage
sites. With over 4,000 external links, it offers rich, well-
categorised and well-presented national coverage, making it a
great source of inspiration for visits or day-trips generally. It
includes very good search facilities which can be restricted to
London, but, sadly, not to free attractions/events only.*

Commercial art galleries
*London remains one of the great centres of the international
market in pictures and objets d'art, and much of the business
is conducted through galleries to which the public has free
access.*
*You could easily spend a week just exploring London's
commercial galleries. As a starting point, the greatest
concentrations of the more traditional operators are found
around Cork Street, Bruton Street and Old Bond Street W1,
and Bury Street and Duke Street SW1. Dealers in more
contemporary works tend to be more widely spread, often in
East London.*

We can't lead you to the changing artistic attractions of the capital, as many of the most interesting commercial shows last for only a month or so. However, help is at hand in the form of an excellent monthly publication – Galleries – of which you can obtain a copy, gratis, from almost any commercial art gallery. Its handy format contains a wealth of information, helpfully organised into areas (with maps) and indexed in every way you could possibly want (including by artist and type of work). It also contains short but interesting articles on many of the forthcoming attractions. Many other publications, such as Time Out, also provide comprehensive listings.

The great auction houses are another fascinating part of the art world – details are given in the Central London section.

Farmers' Markets
www.lfm.org.uk
(020) 7833 0338

Farmers markets offer London consumers the opportunity to buy food direct from the grower or producer – strict guidelines ensure that no one can sell another farmer's produce, and that all goods are produced within 100 miles of London. (London's most famous foodie destination, Borough Market, see page 105, does not come under this category.) Therefore, expect to see only fresh, seasonal (sometimes organic) produce at these lively markets, which often have something of the jollity of French and Italian street markets. The website is the most accurate way to find the times and location of your nearest market, and even gives a calendar of what fruit and vegetables you can expect to find every month. Other produce might include wine, bread, cheeses, honey and fish – look out for free tasters! / Times: vary. Information on the more important general markets is given in the respective area section of the guide.

Parks
One of London's most important charms is its myriad of parks and open spaces. Many of these are listed individually in the relevant sections of this guide. The most famous central parks are managed by the Royal Parks. You can find a lot of information on the 5,000 acres of Crown parkland, and details of forthcoming events, at www.royalparks.org.uk.

The other park-related organisation which punches well above its weight is the Corporation of London. This august body doesn't just manage 150 sites in the Square Mile itself, but also – for historical reasons – over 10,000 acres of green space, woodland and parks elsewhere, including Epping Forest and Hampstead Heath. The City's parks are comprehensively catalogued at www.visitthecity.co.uk.

Londonwide information

Performing arts
www.alternativearts.co.uk
(020) 7375 0441
Alternative Arts is an organisation providing a platform for various performing artists, and which strives to make the arts easily accessible for the general public. Events, generally free, come in all shapes and sizes, and are listed on the website (click on 'programme preview').

For more general arts-related information, see "Art galleries and museums" on page 16.

Waterways
www.waterscape.com
The official website for information on Britain's waterways. Here you will find things to do and places to visit both on the British Waterways network and on other rivers, canals, lakes and reservoirs. Download the 16-page information pack on days-out around London from the websiteto find suggested itineraries, activities, maps, and transport information.

Wildlife
www.wildlondon.org.uk
Harling House, 47-51 Great Suffolk St   (020) 7261 0447
The London Wildlife Trust aims to sustain and enhance London's wildlife habitats, and to this end it manages 57 nature reserves – a free map of locations is available. Each year, more than 600 free indoor and outdoor events, classes and volunteer opportunities are organised – from bat walks to wild flower talks. Visit their website to obtain more information, as well as details and locations of volunteer contacts throughout London.
/ Times: Mon-Fri 9.30am-5.30pm.

Volunteering

Volunteering

Why not pass the time for free, and 'put something back' at the same time? Here are some suggestions:

Age Reminiscence Centre SE3
www.age-exchange.org.uk
11 Blackheath Village   (020) 8318 9105   1–4D
For full details of the Age Reminiscence Centre see page 104. If you like the idea of working with older folk, you might like to consider acting as a volunteer. / Times: Mon-Fri 10am-5pm, Sat 10am -4pm; BR: Blackheath.

BTCV - People Working for a Better Environment N1
www.btcv.org.uk
80 York Way   (020) 7278 4294   4–3C
Get some fresh air, and brush up your 'green' skills with BTCV – the largest organisation in the United Kingdom promoting practical conservation work by volunteers. Its projects range from building footbridges to managing woodland, and volunteers are always welcome. Training is always provided – no experience is necessary. The website gives details of a wide range of courses, access to most of which is free. / Times: Mon-Fri 9am-5pm; Tube: King's Cross.

City Farms BS3
www.farmgarden.org.uk
The Federation of City Farms, The Green House, Hereford St, Bedminster, Bristol   (0117) 923 1800
This organisation holds details of all the city farms and community gardens in Britain – most of which will almost certainly have ongoing requirements for volunteers. Surrey Docks Farm and Spitalfields City Farm are among those always looking for extra help. (See index for a list of London city farms.)

Community Service Volunteers
www.csv.org.uk
237 Pentonville Rd, N1   (020) 7278 6601
Looking for "easy, commitment-free volunteering to suit anyone in London"? Check out the wide-ranging website of Community Service Volunteers, the UK's largest charity devoted to volunteering and training, founded in 1962 by the couple who also founded the (perhaps better-known) VSO (Voluntary Service Overseas).

Gunnersbury Triangle Nature Reserve W4
www.chiswickw4.com
Bollo Ln   (020) 8747 3881   1–3A
This intriguing nature reserve (See entry, page 80) makes use of volunteers in practical management and administrative positions. Interested parties can call or simply turn up. In the summer months there is a programme of events from picnics to adventure quizzes – call ahead for details. / Tube: Chiswick Park; Café, Restaurant, Picnic area.

Heath Hands
Volunteers for Hampstead Heath NW3
www.heath-hands.org.uk
Iveagh Bequest, Kenwood, Hampstead Ln
(020) 8458 9102
Heath Hands is a volunteer group that helps the Corporation of London make Hampstead Heath (even) greener. Activities include garden maintenance, tree work and bird box construction. The organisation is happy to welcome helpers who are only able to assist for a day or two – you must call in advance to make sure there are enough tools on the day you wish to help out. Volunteers must be at least 16 years old. See Wildlife entry on page 18. / Café, Picnic area.

Thames 21 Project
www.thames21.org.uk
(020) 7248 7171
Set up in 1998, the Project's aim is to improve and enhance the environment of London's rivers, and it removes hundreds of tons of litter annually. If you're interested in helping out – on a regular or 'one-off' basis – visit the website or call the number given.

Shane Global Village W1
www.shaneglobal.com
59 South Molton St   (020) 7499 8533   2–2B
Need to learn (or improve your) English for free? Why not embark on a four-week course in central London. Every four weeks a new intake of teachers (on a month-long programme leading to a recognised qualification of teaching English as a foreign language, TEFL) need a class to practise on. Around 15 places are available for instruction at elementary and intermediate levels. Would-be students must commit themselves for the full duration and pay a £20 deposit which is returned on completion of the course. / Times: Mon-Fri 2pm-4pm; Tube: Bond Street.

Thrive
www.thrive.org.uk
(020) 7720 2212
Founded in 1978, this national charity uses 'therapeutic horticulture' to improve the lives of disabled, disadvantaged and older people. Volunteers are always required to work in the gardens – no gardening experience is necessary. The current London project is in Battersea.

Waterway Recovery Group
www.wrg.org.uk
PO Box 114, Rickmansworth   (01923) 711114
A volunteer organisation helping to restore derelict canals. Wish to be kept abreast of the 'dirty weekend' possibilities (as they call them)? – just register on the website.

Events

Regular events

Ceremony of the Keys EC3

www.hrp.org.uk

Tower of London   (0844) 482 7777

In accordance with seven centuries of tradition, the Tower of London (home, of course, to the Crown Jewels) is secured for the night with a 10 minute ceremony. Anyone can apply for a ticket to attend, but you need to do so in writing enclosing an SAE (Ceremony of the Keys, The Operations Department, HM Tower of London, London EC3N 4AB) stating the names and addresses of those in your group and the date you would like to attend, giving at least two months' notice. / Times: nightly at 9.30pm; Tube: Tower Hill.

Changing the Guard (Buckingham Palace) SW1

www.royal.gov.uk

The changing of the sentries at Buckingham Palace is famous around the world. The new guard leaves Wellington Barracks three minutes before the change, and, preceded by a band, marches down Birdcage Walk to the palace. The ceremony lasts 40 minutes, and takes place inside the railings of the palace itself. The event is subject to cancellation in very bad weather or during state visits. In conjunction with this event, the St. James's Palace detachment of the Queen's Guard marches to Buckingham Palace at 11.15am and back to St. James's Palace at 12.10pm. / Times: 11.30am daily (Nov-Mar open every other day); Tube: Green Park.

Changing the Guard (Horse Guards) SW1

www.royal.gov.uk

Horse Guards Parade

In a daily burst of pageantry, a mounted guard leaves Hyde Park Barracks at 10.28am (Sun 9.28am) and proceeds, via Hyde Park Corner and Constitution Hill, to arrive at Horse Guards Parade at 11am (Sun 10am), where the guard is changed. If you want to see a truly romantic London sight, you won't do better than the splendidly attired mounted guardsmen making their way through Hyde Park. / Times: 11am daily (Sun 10am); Tube: Hyde Park Corner, St James's Park.

Gun Salutes

www.royalparks.org.uk

(020) 7298 2000

One of the most striking sights in London is the gun salutes which hail royal and state events. These take place in Green, St James's or Hyde Park (12 noon) and at the Tower of London (1pm) on the following dates (or, if a Sun, the next day): 6 February (Accession Day); 21 April (the Queen's birthday); 2 June (Coronation Day); and 10 June (the Duke of Edinburgh's birthday). Salutes also mark state visits (usually in May and October), Trooping the Colour (June) and the State Opening of Parliament (October or November). Details of these and other events in the Royal Parks are given in the Summer Entertainment Programme available with an A5 SAE from the Old Police House, Hyde Park, London W2 2UH (tel (020) 7298 2000). / Tube: Hyde Park Corner, Tower Hill.

Annual timetable

Barely a month goes by in London without some great event happening which can provide a good focus for a day out, especially with children in tow. The major events which happen on an annual basis are as follows.

January

London Parade
www.londonparade.co.uk
(0900) 525 2020 (recorded information)
The New Year starts with a bang as an American-style family event takes place on the first day of the year. Hundreds of thousands of people turn out to see the big parade, which includes 6,000 majorettes (flown in from the States), clowns, floats and dance displays. It starts from Parliament Square at noon and the final band reaches Berkeley Square in Mayfair around 3pm. The procession (for which Whitehall or Piccadilly offers the best vantage point) consists of marching bands, floats and horse-drawn carriages, in which ride the Archbishop and Lord Mayor of Westminster and mayors of all the London boroughs (but not, of course, the fiercely independent City, which has its own Big Day, the Lord Mayor's Show, in November). / Tube: Westminster, St James's Park, Green Park.

Chinese New Year
www.london.gov.uk
In late January or early February, Chinatown celebrates the Chinese New Year with noisy, colourful parades (including the famous papier mâché dragons), which last most of the day (11am-6.30pm). The whole area (around Gerrard Street W1) is brightly decorated for the event. / Tube: Leicester Square.

Events

Pancake Day Races
Covent Garden WC2/ Spitalfields Market E1
(020) 7375 0441 (Alternative Arts)
*Shrove Tuesday ('Pancake Day') sees traditional races between
pancake-tossing relay-teams at Spitalfields (12.30pm).*
/ Tube: Liverpool Street.

Head of the River Race
www.horr.co.uk
(01932) 220401
*The Oxford and Cambridge Boat Race may be more famous,
but, for the casual observer, the Head of the River Race, rowed
on a Sat in March from Mortlake to Putney, is probably a more
interesting rowing race to watch. The sheer number of crews
(usually over 400) means that the colourful procession of eight-
oared boats (which are set off 10 seconds apart) takes well
over an hour. Being a timed race, however, it does have the
disadvantage that no one knows who has won until it's all over.
Best vantage points are as for the Boat Race (below), but those
in the know go to Chiswick Bridge to watch the pre-race
marshalling of hundreds of boats in a confined stretch of the
river. Start times vary according to the tides. / Tube: Putney Bridge;
Picnic area.*

Oxford & Cambridge Boat Race
www.theboatrace.org
*It may be an arcane and thoroughly English way of spending an
afternoon, but the world's most famous boat race, between
Oxford and Cambridge University Boat Clubs, continues to
exercise an extraordinary grip on the popular imagination. Tens
of thousands of people turn out every year to snatch a passing
glimpse of an 18-minute race (first rowed on the Thames in
1830) which, from a practical point of view, is much better
watched on television. The best vantage points for the four-mile
race from Putney to Mortlake are generally held to be at the
half-way point (Hammersmith) or at the finish – but you don't
get much of a view anywhere and the real point is not the race
but the atmosphere. Take a picnic and – if you want to know
who's won – a radio. / Tube: Hammersmith, Putney Bridge.*

April

Flora London Marathon

www.london-marathon.co.uk

(020) 7902 0200

The London Marathon, first run in 1981 (and sponsored since 1996 by Flora) is one of the world's major marathons. It has grown into a huge event which attracts nearly 40,000 runners and over half a million spectators annually. Its sheer scale and spectacle makes it a good family day out. Over half of the runners are taking part for charity. Many run in costume, and you may see some famous faces. The course of just over 26 miles begins (around 9am) in Greenwich Park and ends (having taken a circuitous route) outside Buckingham Palace. The leading runners take a little over two hours to complete the course, but the stragglers make it practically an all-day event.

Streatham Common Kite Day SE3

www.streathamkiteday.org.uk

Streatham Common   (020) 8764 9655

London's best-established annual kite festival takes place around Easter – check out the website to confirm dates and other details. It makes a good day out for all the family.
/ BR: Streatham or Stretham Common.

May

Canalway Cavalcade W9

www.waterways.org.uk

Pool of Little Venice, Paddington   (01494) 783453

Watercrafts of all types take part in the colourful boat rally organised by the Inland Waterways Association. In conjunction with the rally, this lively family event boasts live music, Morris dancing, a teddy bears picnic, boat trips and waterway-related trade and craft stalls. An evening highlight is the illuminated boat procession which takes place on the Sun. / Times: May Day bank hol weekend, 10am-6pm and Sun eve; Tube: Warwick Avenue.

Coin Street Festival SE1

www.coinstreet.org

Gabriel's Wharf, Bernie Spain Gardens, Oxo Tower Wharf

(020) 7928 0960

A popular South Bank event that runs from mid-June to September, and which celebrates the many cultures and interests of the people who live, work in, or visit the capital. Highlights are live music and street performances – from French street theatre, perhaps, to African storytelling – and there are many activities for children, including workshops and competitions. Almost every weekend there is a day of events, all of which are free, usually around a particular theme – see website for details. / Tube: Waterloo, Blackfriars, Southwark.

Events

May Fayre & Puppet Festival WC2

www.alternativearts.co.uk
St Paul's Church & Gardens, Bedford St
(020) 7375 0441 (Alternative Arts)
This all-day event, which takes place on the Sun nearest to 9 May, celebrates the art of puppetry, with Punch and Judy performers from all over the country. There's a 'Grand Procession' at 10.30am, and stalls and activities for the rest of the day. / Times: 10.30am-5.30pm daily; Tube: Covent Garden, Leicester Square.

June

City of London Festival* EC2

www.colf.org
Fitz Eylwin House, 25 Holborn Viaduct
(020) 7583 3585
In late June/early July, the City enjoys an explosion of music. If you're looking for free events, seek out the world music series which takes place on weekday lunchtimes at venues throughout the Square Mile — workers and tourists alike are entertained by street theatre and dance, jazz, Latin and brass bands. There is almost invariably a charge for the evening events. For full listings and timetables, see the website.

Devizes to Westminster International Canoe Race

www.dwrace.org.uk
(0118) 966 5912
Often referred to as the 'Canoeist's Everest', this claims to be the world's toughest canoe race, lasting for three days and 125 miles (the course must be completed in under 100 hours). It has been raced every Easter since 1948, along the Kennet and Avon Canal to Reading, where it enters the Thames. You can watch the end of the race, at Westminster Bridge (usually around 9am on Mon morning) from the relative comfort of the Embankment.

Greenwich & Docklands International Festival*

www.festival.org
(020) 8305 1818
This multi-arts extravaganza (which generally takes place in late-June) now spans both banks of the Thames (and much of east London). Many of the attractions are free, and include opening and closing night pyrotechnics, open-air music and dance performances. For details, you can visit the website or ring the festival hotline. / Tube: Greenwich, Woolwich (DLR).

Henley Royal Regatta*

www.hrr.co.uk
(01491) 572153
tourist info (01491) 578034
Henley, established in 1839, is the world's oldest major rowing regatta. It takes place in late June/early July (the final Sun is always the 27th Sun of the year). Even if you've never been in a rowing boat in your life, and even if you don't know anyone

*who is a member of one of the enclosures, it's still one of the
most enjoyable events of the 'Season' and manages, to an
extraordinary extent, to maintain something of the atmosphere
of an Edwardian garden party. Take a picnic, arrive early, and
find a good viewpoint along the towpath – all but the last third
of a mile or so of the course is open to the public, and at many
points you can hear the commentary. The event lasts from
Wed to Sun – it's much less crowded on the weekdays.*
/ BR: Henley on Thames.

Pride London*
www.pridelondon.org
*London's major gay and lesbian festival takes place in late
June/early July. Abandon any thoughts that this is a 'minority'
event – it's one of the biggest celebrations of the year, with the
police reckoning that the parade and associated events (not all
free) attracted over 800,000 people in 2008.*

Spitalfields Summer Festival* E1
www.spitalfieldsfestival.org.uk
75 Brushfield St   (020) 7377 0287
*Spitalfields plays host to two music festivals annually – in
summer and another one just before Christmas. The festivals
offer a varied programme of lunchtime and evening concerts of
music from c15 to contemporary. There are also exhibitions
and a fringe festival, including arts events, comedy and circus
performances. Some events, only, are free of charge – there is
(for once!) a dedicated link to these events on the home page
of the website.* / Tube: Shoreditch, Liverpool Street, Aldgate East.

The Scoop SE1
www.morelondon.com
The Queen's Walk   (020) 7403 4866   5–4D
*The Scoop at More London is an outdoor amphitheatre which
seats 800 people. In the the summer there are various free
events such as films, music, theatre and local community
activities. Their events include the "Fringe" festival in June,
lunchtime and evening music performances in July, and two
theatre shows for the month of August. Check website for
details.* / Tube: London Bridge.

Trooping the Colour*
www.trooping-the-colour.co.uk
(020) 7414 2479
*A Sat in early June sees the celebration of the Queen's Official
Birthday, when she inspects an elaborate military display at
Horse Guards Parade SW1. At 1pm, after her return to
Buckingham Palace, there is an RAF flypast down the Mall.*

*There is a charge to attend the event itself (although, of
course, you can freely watch the procession down the Mall and
the flypast), but tickets for the two rehearsals are allocated,*

without any charge, by ballot. Apply in January or February, with an SAE, to Brigade Major (Trooping the Colour), Headquarters, Household Division, Horse Guards, Whitehall London SW1A 2AX.

For exhaustive information, and pictures, see the (unofficial) website, whose address we have given. / *Tube: St James's Park.*

West End Live WC2
www.westendlive.co.uk
Leicester Sq (020) 7641 5370
A summer event, held in Leicester Square, attracting around 200,000 visitors throughout the weekend. The event includes edited highlights from theatre shows, participatory activities and small exhibitions drawn from museums, galleries and other attractions. / *Tube: Leicester Square.*

July

Croydon Summer Festival*
www.croydonfestival.com
(020) 8253 1030
A classic free day out for all the family, including a wide range of live music – Caribbean and Latin – as well as jazz. A highlight is the Croydon Mela, London's second largest Asian music festival. A full brochure of events is available approximately two months prior to the festival, which lasts for two weeks in July. / *Café.*

Doggett's Coat & Badge Race
www.watermenshall.org
The oldest event in British sport, this sculling (two-oared rowing) race takes place from Chelsea to London Bridge (or, to be precise, the Coat and Badge pub). It was in 1751 that Thomas Dogget, an Irish actor and comedian, funded the first race, to commemorate the accession of George I. It was originally restricted to 'professional watermen' only, but the rules have been relaxed to permit amateurs in recent years.

Hillingdon Borough Carnival
www.hillingdon.gov.uk
Hayes, Middx (01895) 250029
Every year the second Sat in July sees the streets of Hayes erupt with floats and crowds. Up to 20 floats, followed by marching bands, lead the way from Pump Lane at 12.30pm, to Barra Hall Park. Here you will find a funfair, Punch and Judy shows, clowns, stalls, pony rides, live music, stilt-walking, gladiators and impersonators. / *BR: Hayes and Harlington.*

Swan Upping
www.royal.gov.uk
(020) 7236 1863

All the swans on the Thames between London Bridge and Henley belong to the Queen or one of two City livery companies: the Dyers and the Vintners. This cosy three-way arrangement has been in place since 1510. Each year, it is necessary to mark the cygnets to show to whom they belong (which depends on who owns their parents). This task is carried out every third week of July, by a procession of six 'Thames Skiffs' (rowed by colourfully-uniformed oarsmen), which takes a week to progress from Sunbury to Abingdon Bridge. When swans are spotted, the traditional cry of "All-up" is raised, and they are corralled by three skiffs, one staffed by each of the potential owners, in preparation for identification and marking. The swans, it seems, do not always come quietly. If you want to know when and where you can witness this extraordinary ritual, call the Vintners on the number given. Traditionally, swans were marked by nicking their bills, but they are now ringed instead – in deference to tradition, the practice is, of course, known as 'nicking'.

August

Notting Hill Carnival
www.nottinghillcarnival.biz
(020) 7727 0072

The August bank holiday sees the largest street party in Europe – over a million people attending a musical celebration of Afro-Caribbean culture. The carnival is centred around the northern parts of the Portobello Road. Sun sees the Children's Carnival Day, while the main procession of floats takes place on Mon. There is music for all tastes, including reggae, jazz, hip-hop and house. The whole event is certainly impressive in its sheer scale and vitality, but this may make it seem rather daunting to some people. All the common-sense rules of attending such a large and crowded occasion apply – don't drive there, keep hold of children, carry as little money as possible, and don't hang around once the daytime festivities are over. Leave your English reserve at home, and the music and atmosphere might well transport you to the Caribbean! (NB By the time this guide went to press, it had not finally been confirmed that the Carnival would carry on in 2009 and beyond.) / Tube: Notting Hill Gate, Ladbroke Grove.

September

Thames Festival
www.thamesfestival.org
Victoria Embankment and South Bank by OXO Tower
(020) 7928 8998

From Frost Fairs to GLC Thames Days, London's river has long been a natural focal point for pageantry and celebrations. The Thames Festival – described by the Evening Standard as

"London's biggest end-of-summer party" — continues the tradition. It takes place in many locations on the South Bank, and involves a whole host of musical and other events, waterborne and not. In short, it really is a classic day out for all the family, ending with a thumping firework display. Check out the website for a list of events, and a map. / Times: 2nd or 3rd weekend in Sep (Sat and Sun); Tube: Waterloo, Southwark, Blackfriars; Café.

Angel Canal Festival N1

City Road Basin, Regent's Canal, off Wharf Rd
This annual community festival celebrates the Regent's Canal in Islington, and is based around City Road Lock and Basin. Always held on the first Sun in September, the festival features a variety of stalls, a funfair, music, street theatre, boat trips and a regatta. Some activities are ticketed, though admission to the festival is free. / Times: 11am-5pm daily; Tube: Angel.

Great River Race

www.greatriverrace.co.uk
(020) 8398 9057 c/o Stuart Wolff
This ever more popular event has all the ingredients of a Great British Success Story. For a start, the idea behind it is completely — inspiringly — batty. Take more than 250 oared boats (rule: no racing-boats allowed), devise a handicapping system (which allows some boats to start 100 minutes before others) and set them off (down a tidal river) on a 22-mile journey from Ham House in Richmond to Island Gardens on the Isle of Dogs. The event attracts every type of boat (from Chinese dragon boats to Hawaiian war canoes) and rowers and paddlers of all ages and of every degree of seriousness, from all over the world. It's a wonderful spectacle, and one which can be viewed from any London bank of the Thames, though the greatest excitement is of course at the start, at Richmond, (3.30pm) and the finish: best viewing by the Cutty Sark, in Greenwich (6.45pm). / Tube: choice of 12 riverside stations between Richmond and Island Gardens (DLR).

Heritage Open Days

www.heritageopendays.org.uk
(020) 7539 7918
The Civic Trust co-ordinates an annual exercise which allows the public to see, for free, buildings of historic or architectural interest that are usually closed to general enquirers. The celebration takes place in the second weekend of September and highlights various properties, from windmills to music halls, throughout England. For details of the buildings that will be open, write to: Heritage Open Days, The Civic Trust, Essex Hall, 1-6 Essex Street, London WC2R 3HU, enclosing six second class stamps. Or check out the website.

London Open House
www.londonopenhouse.org
(020) 3006 7008

Heritage Open Day (see above) is a national event. The London equivalent takes place a week later. On these dates the public can gain free admittance to all types of buildings, from cinemas and colleges to theatres, even perhaps a former mortuary, which are not normally accessible. Over 500 buildings are open. There are also walks, exhibitions and lectures. The idea is to celebrate London's wealth of architecture, to promote public awareness of architecture and the built environment and to encourage civic pride. In addition, there are building tours and activities specifically designed for children. For details, look for leaflets in galleries around town or check the website.

Raising of the Thames Barrier SE18
www.environment-agency.gov.uk
Unity Way   (020) 8854 1373

Canute was wrong – you can hold back the tide, but only by spending half a billion pounds on a great river barrier, designed to protect central London from the ever-growing risk of flooding. Completed in 1982, the Thames Barrier (see also, South London) is a miracle of modern engineering. Once a year (usually in September or October) there is an all-day test and the massive steel gates are either raised or dropped against the high tide. There are also tests each month, but these take place as early in the morning as tides permit and (because it involves closing a working river) for as short a period as possible. Check out the website for details.
/ Times: 10.30am-4.30pm (Sep-Mar 11am-3.30pm); BR: Charlton; Café.

October_____

Diwali
Funfairs and fireworks take place in Ealing and Hounslow in October (or early November) to mark one of the largest festivals celebrating Hindus, Sikhs and Jains. Check press for details. Local councils often organise festivals.

Punch & Judy Festival WC2
www.punchandjudyfellowship.org.uk
Covent Garden   (020) 7836 9136

The first Sun of October sees a plethora of Punch and Judy shows, and their continental equivalents – Polichinelle (France), Kasper (Germany) and Pulcinella (Italy). / Tube: Leicester Square.

Events

St George in Southwark Festival
www.stgeorgefestival.org.uk
(020) 7403 7400
A multicultural festival commemorating England's patron saint. Past festivals have included performances by local theatre groups, talks by local historians, guided tours of the Cathedral (patron, St. George), storytelling in the Children's Library, and other activities honouring the saint. A full guide to the festival can be viewed on the website. / Tube: Southwark, London Bridge, Borough.

State Opening of Parliament
www.parliament.uk
If you want to see the Queen wearing a crown and riding in a gilded coach, the only annual opportunity to do so is the State Opening of Parliament (date varies). Her Majesty rides from Buckingham Palace to Westminster to deliver the Queen's Speech (which sets out the Government's legislative plans for the forthcoming year, and is, in fact, written by the Prime Minister) and then returns to her palace. There are accompanying gun salutes at Green Park and the Tower of London. As an event, it's not hugely well attended, and offers possibly the best 'royal-watching' opportunity of the year. / Tube: Westminster.

Trafalgar Day Parade WC2
Trafalgar Sq
A commemoration service for Nelson's 1805 victory at Trafalgar takes place on the nearest Sun to 21 October. Wreaths are laid at Nelson's Column by over 500 Sea Cadets. / Tube: Leicester Square, Charing Cross.

November

RAC London to Brighton Veteran Car Run
www.vccofgb.co.uk/lontobri/index.htm
Sat 14 November 1896 was a great day in the history of British motoring – for the first time it was legal to proceed at more than 4mph and without being preceded by a man with a red flag (the new speed limit was set at a staggering 14mph). Ever since (war years excepted), horseless carriages have taken part in an annual celebration of automobile 'Emancipation'. The spectacle now attracts over a million spectators a year. The Run – it is NOT a race – takes place on the first Sun in November, leaving Hyde Park at 7.30am, and progressing via Westminster (7.35am) and Lambeth Town Hall (7.45am) to Madeira Drive, Brighton, where the frontrunners arrive around 10.30am. (Times are provisional – check website.) Only cars built before 1905 are eligible to take part, and competitors come from all over the world. / Tube: Hyde Park Corner.

Fireworks Night

The annual remembrance of the failure of the Gunpowder Plot (when Guy Fawkes and his merry men attempted, in 1605, to blow up monarch, lords and commoners assembled at Westminster) is celebrated with a large number of bonfire and firework parties of all sizes all over London. Parties take place on November 5 and, if it falls mid-week, the weekends before and after. The larger events are widely advertised on posters and in local newspapers. Many, but not all, are free – contributions, however, are often welcome.

Lord Mayor's Show

www.lordmayorsshow.org

The Lord Mayor's Show has taken place – plague permitting – in some form in most years since 1215. It celebrates the annual presentation of the new Lord Mayor of London to the Queen's Justices. This formerly took place at Westminster, but now involves a rather shorter journey to the Royal Courts of Justice in the Strand. The show takes place on the second Sat of November, and begins at the Guildhall at 11am with a one-and-a-half-mile long procession, which includes 200 horses, 60 floats, 20 bands and about 6,000 people. The centrepiece of the procession is the Lord Mayor's gilded, c18 coach (housed for the rest of the year in the Museum of London), pulled by six shire horses. This is a great traditional Londoners' day out – a whole day's entertainment is provided, ending with a firework display over the Thames – and about a half of a million people attend annually. Many City attractions, generally closed at weekends, open on the day of the show. / Tube: Bank.

Remembrance Sunday SW1

Whitehall

The Sun nearest to 11 November sees the most sober, and the most moving, large-scale event of the year. Just after 11am, the Queen and representatives of the government and the Commonwealth lay wreaths of Flanders poppies on the Cenotaph to commemorate those who gave their lives in war. After the short service, the tone becomes a little lighter as the veterans march past. / Tube: Embankment, Charing Cross, Westminster.

December

Christmas Tree WC2

www.london.gov.uk

Trafalgar Sq

The great Christmas Tree in Trafalgar Square, decorated with its bright white lamps, is an annual gift from the people of Oslo to the people of London. There are regular carol concerts around the tree. / Tube: Charing Cross.

Christmas Lights

The heartland of London's shopping – Oxford Street, Regent Street and Bond Street – has put on an improving festive show in recent years (if not quite up to, say, the Champs-Elysées). Carnaby Street also joins in, usually with some fairly avant-garde variations on the festive theme. The lights are given a

celebrity 'switch on' in November, and they are there to be
admired until Twelfth Night. An evening visit to this part of
town also permits some vigorous window-shopping at Selfridges
and the other stores of Oxford Street, and Hamleys and Liberty
on Regent Street. Fortnum & Mason on Piccadilly usually puts
on a particularly good seasonal display. Don't forget that, in the
run-up to Christmas, the whole of the West End can be
surprisingly crowded well after the shops have closed.
/ Tube: Marble Arch, Oxford Circus, Bond Street, Piccadilly Circus.

Spitalfields Winter Festival* E1
www.spitalfieldsfestival.org.uk
Shoreditch Church, Shoreditch High St   (020) 7377 0287
See the Summer Festival (June) for details. The Winter Festival
– apart from the obvious Christmas theme and carol singing –
is very similar. / Times: details from hotline or website; Tube: Old Street,
Liverpool Street.

New Year's Eve
Packing yourself into Trafalgar Square was traditionally the way
to see in the New Year in London, but in recent times the focus
of celebrations has moved to a great firework display by the
Thames (and centred in most recent years on the London Eye).
Those who do not like crowds should definitely stay away, and
even those who do should think twice – even the Powers That
Be, who put on the display, are getting concerned that it's just
too popular. Getting home is, unusually, free of charge as
London Transport operates its annual (usually sponsored) offer
of free transport throughout the capital, with the tubes running
well past midnight. If you'd like to consider an alternative, you
could spend the evening spanning two hemispheres – the
Greenwich and Docklands Festival (see above for details and
website) organise a free New Year's Eve event called First
Night, with fireworks and street entertainments, centred on
Greenwich town centre.

Entertainments

Radio & Television

BBC TV and radio W12
www.bbc.co.uk/tickets
BBC Studio Audiences, PO Box 3000   (0370) 901 1227
*Want to get tickets for some of Britain's best-known shows?
The BBC's website has an excellent booking facility which lets
you book tickets for many of its TV and radio programmes, and
all at no cost to yourself at all. You can even browse what's
available by reference to your preferred date and venue. The
problem, of course, is that some of the shows are very popular
indeed, so you'd better be quick off the mark.*

*Note, incidentally, the useful but very powerful link: "Can't find
what you're looking for?", which is hidden away at the bottom
of the search results. This leads you through to a cornucopia of
further delights which, for various reasons, don't get listed by
the main online booking facility.*

TV – independents
*Who'd have thought, in this funny old world, that a company
could want to proclaim that it was "The No. 1 official free
television and radio audience ticket destination". Well, that's
the proud boast of www.applausestore.co.uk – a very smart
website offering tickets to a whole host of shows. Other rather
similar sites, albeit offering a smaller range of shows, are
www.sroaudiences.com and www.tvrecordings.com. Hat Trick
Productions – popular for some of the more celebrated shows
of recent times – recruits audiences for its various shows via its
own website www.hattrick.co.uk. For further inspiration, consult:
www.itv.com/BeonTV/Tickets*

Music

City music
www.cityevents.co.uk & www.colf.org
*There is music in one of the many churches of the City almost
every lunchtime – concerts usually begin between 1pm and
1.15pm and generally last no more than an hour. A useful
monthly publication, City Events, available from the City of
London Information Centre by St Paul's, gives advance details,
or you can check online. Alternatively, if you arrive at the
centre by 12.40pm you should have time to locate the concert
of your choice and walk to the appropriate church.*

*The top time of year for City music is during the City of London
Festival (see also) in late June/early July.*

*The Corporation of London also presents a series of band
concerts through the summer at three locations (Finsbury
Circus, Tower Place and Royal Exchange Forecourt) from noon
to 2pm (Jul-Aug) – you can get a leaflet from the Information
Centre for dates and times. / Tube: Bank, St Paul's.*

City Music Society EC2

www.citymusicsociety.org
Bishopsgate Institute Great Hall, 230 Bishopsgate
(020) 8542 0950   5–1D
Founded in 1943, the City Music Society was inspired by Dame Myra Hess's concerts during World War II. The Society presents around 26 concerts per year and has free lunchtime concerts from September to March (every Tue at 1.05pm, sometimes with pre-concert talks beginning at 12.15pm).
/ Tube: Liverpool Street.

Music in the Royal Parks

www.royalparks.org.uk
(020) 7298 2000
Many of the Royal Parks (Hyde, Regent's, St James's, Green, Greenwich and Richmond, and Kensington Gardens) offer music (and other events) on a regular basis (especially, of course, in summer). The attractions (clearly flagged where 'free') are all set out on the What's On section of the website. You can also register online to receive a (hard-copy) newsletter.

Notting Hill Arts Club W11

www.nottinghillartsclub.com
21 Notting Hill Gate   (020) 7460 4459   1–3B
The club holds regular music and arts events and exhibitions including "RoTa" which has been running every Sat since 2001. This event runs from 4pm-6pm and features three or four live bands and DJ's. Other concerts include "Free Wheeler" which is held every other month, and "Death Disco" each Wed night which features two bands. They also hold art exhibitions (with a graphic design focus) which can usually be visited without charge during the "early bird" window from 6pm-8pm. Visit the website for details. / Tube: Notting Hill Gate.

Royal Opera House* WC2

www.roh.org.uk
Covent Garden   (020) 7304 4000 (Box office)   2–2D
In addition to the imposing main auditorium, the Royal Opera House has several 'spaces', one of which is the Linbury Studio Theatre, where free chamber music concerts are given on Mon at 1pm. Visitors to the Opera House are also able to see the impressive foyer areas and view permanent displays and temporary exhibitions situated around the building. (Some areas may be unavailable if events are taking place during the day.)

Look out also for live summertime relays from the main auditorium to a big screen in the piazza. / Times: Opera House from 10am; Vilar Floral Hall 10am-3.30pm; Tube: Covent Garden.

South Bank Centre SE1

www.southbankcentre.co.uk
Belvedere Rd   (0871) 663 2500   2–3D
See website for details of performances around this impressive, post-war South Bank building. / Times: Royal Festival Hall 10am-11pm daily; Gallery 10am-6pm daily; Waterloo or Embankment.

Entertainments

The Temple Church EC4
www.templemusic.org
Fleet St   (020) 7427 5640   5–2A
This c12 church holds lunchtime organ recitals every Wed from 1.15pm-1.45pm. / Tube: Temple, Blackfriars.

Music colleges

London boasts some of the finest music colleges in the world and, to those who enjoy classical music, they represent an extremely fertile source of free entertainment.

All the schools listed give three or four concerts or recitals a week during their term times. The most popular performances tend to be the larger ones – those with symphony orchestras or pieces with a large chorus – of which there may be five or so in a term at any given school.

Guildhall School of Music & Drama* EC2
www.gsmd.ac.uk
Barbican, Silk St   (020) 7382 7192   5–1C
Opera, jazz, ensemble, contemporary music... performances, most of which are free, take place at the School, at the Barbican, and elsewhere, lunchtimes and evenings. They're detailed online, or you can ask for the hard-copy termly programme of events. / Tube: Moorgate, Barbican.

Royal Academy of Music NW1
www.ram.ac.uk
Marylebone Rd   (020) 7873 7300   2–1A
Details of some ten free events a week are listed on the website, or in the termly Diary of Events (available from the box office on the number given). In general, lunchtime concerts take place Tue-Thu at 1.05pm in the foyer, while early-evening concerts take place on Tue at 5.05pm in the Duke's Hall. In addition, there are various other evening concerts, showcasing classical, jazz and chamber music. There is also a chamber music series called Free on Fridays which is designed to show off the Academy's best performers. The concerts begin at 1.05pm and last about an hour. Visit the website for events and exhibitions. / Tube: Baker Street; Café.

Royal College of Music SW7
www.rcm.ac.uk
Prince Consort Rd   (020) 7589 3643 ext 4380   3–1B
Most performances are given at the college, just behind the Royal Albert Hall, although quite a number are held at other venues around the capital. For example, at 1.05pm on Fri during term time, a concert is given at the imposing Church of St Mary Abbots in the centre of Kensington (tube: High Street Kensington). Lunchtime concerts take place variously in the Recital Hall, the Concert Hall and St Mary Abbots – check the website or ring for details. / Tube: South Kensington.

Trinity College of Music* SE10
www.tcm.ac.uk
King Charles Court, Old Royal Naval College, Greenwich
(020) 8305 3888   2–1A
*In addition to performances, there are occasional musical
competitions and large-scale concerts. Concerts and recitals
take place in the college (generally at 1pm), as well as the
Regency Hall and churches around London. Not all are free –
check the website. / Tube: Bond Street.*

Comedy

Comedy Café* EC2
www.comedycafe.co.uk
66/68 Rivington St   (020) 7739 5706   5–1D
*The Comedy Café in Shoreditch is one of the few purpose-built
comedy clubs in London. If you would like to sample some of
the stand up for free, visit the "Open Mike Nights" held every
Wed. / Tube: Old St, Liverpool St.*

Lectures

British Academy SW1
www.britac.ac.uk
10 Carlton House Terrace   (020) 7969 5200   2–3C
*Specialising in humanities and social sciences, the British
Academy was established by Royal Charter in 1902, and is now
composed of 900 distinguished scholars. They hold 23 lecture
series and annual events relating to the humanities and social
sciences, all of which are listed on the website with instructions
on booking tickets. / Tube: Charing Cross.*

Gresham College EC1
www.gresham.ac.uk
Barnard's Inn Hall   (020) 7831 0575   5–2A
*Gresham College was founded by Sir Thomas Gresham, a c16
Lord Mayor. For over 400 years Gresham Professors have given
free public lectures, currently by eight professors. Topics might
be as various as Ronald Reagan's presidency and London's role
in navigation. / Tube: Chancery Lane.*

London School of Economics WC2
www.lse.ac.uk
Houghton St   (020) 7955 6043   2–2D
*LSE holds a public lecture programme with over 100 lectures
each term. Recent speakers include leading politicians and
academics such as Alan Greenspan of the US Federal Reserve.
Unless otherwise stated, all events on the regularly updated
LSE events website are free and open to the public. Lectures
usually occur in the early evening and last one and a half
hours. / Tube: Holborn.*

Entertainments

Royal Society of Arts* WC2
www.thersa.org
8 John Adam St   (020) 7930 5115   2–2C
The Royal Society for the Encouragement of Arts, Manufactures and Commerce (to give it its full name) is located just off the Strand, in a fine house that was designed for the Society by Robert Adam in the 1770s. The RSA provides one of the biggest free events programmes in the UK with over 150 lectures between September and July. They also hold weekly Thu lunch lectures. All events are free and open to the public (but book ahead of time as they fill up). Recent speakers include Kofi Annan and Al Gore. Visit the website to book tickets. / Times: 1st Sun of month (except Jan) from 10am-1pm; Tube: Embankment, Charing Cross.

University College London Lunch Hour Lectures WC1
www.ucl.ac.uk/lhl
University College London, Gower St
(020) 7679 7675   2–1C
UCL's professors give free lectures during the Spring and Autumn terms in the College's Darwin Theatre. Subjects might range from 'The Descent of Man' to 'War – The Future of Twentieth Century Conflict' and are open to all. Check the website for details. / Times: Tue and Thu 1.15pm-1.55pm; Tube: Goodge Street, Euston Square.

Other activities

Courts
www.hmcourts-service.gov.uk
If you have half a day to kill, you might find it interesting, and perhaps amusing, to spend it in court. There are surprisingly three types of court which will be within easy reach of most parts of London – Magistrates, Crown and County Courts.

All human life passes through London's magistrates courts, where the highest and the lowest appear to explain why they have (or have not) committed minor criminal offences, from drunkenness to speeding. Sometimes it will be pretty humdrum stuff (if not without human interest), but if you hit lucky, you may experience a real trial, probably not lasting more than a day, where the question "did he (or she) do it?" is of more than academic interest, especially to the person in the dock.

In the Crown courts, the more serious crimes – all the way up to murder – are tried by a bewigged judge and a jury. The disadvantage for the casual visitor is that most trials go on for several days, so inevitably you will see only a fraction of the proceedings. By far the most interesting theatre is to be found when a witness (especially the defendant) is being cross-examined by the opposing side's counsel. The Old Bailey (see The City) is London's senior Crown court.

County Courts resolve civil disputes (such as claims for damages, perhaps arising from a motor accident or unpaid debts). Again, cross-examination is generally by far the most gripping part of a trial. The most important civil trials take place at the Royal Courts of Justice (see The City).

For the address of your local court, consult the telephone directory. Courts generally sit between 10am and 4.30pm. Children under 16 are not usually admitted into the public galleries.

Central London

Introduction

The fact that Central London is at the ceremonial and governmental heart of Britain – comprising as it does the **Houses of Parliament**, **Westminster Abbey**, **Buckingham Palace** and 10 Downing Street – provides an almost unequalled range of famous historic attractions. The Abbey and Parliament can be visited, but only with a degree of planning.

Another major theme is art and antiquities – this area contains some of the most significant museums and art galleries in the world, such as the **British Museum** and the **National Gallery**. There are, however, also smaller attractions with first-rate collections – among these the **Wallace Collection** and **Sir John Soane's Museum** stand out. In addition, the commercial art world provides a huge and ever-changing selection of pictures and objects to view, and the institutions which deal in them have their own special interest and charm. A visit to one of the great auctioneers, **Sotheby's** or **Christie's**, combines art with theatre. (For a guide to the commercial galleries, see page 16).

Central London is a window-shopper's paradise, containing as it does most of the UK's top shops – ranging from **Harrods**, **Selfridges** and **Fortnum & Mason** at the larger end of the scale to the opulent boutiques of **Old Bond Street**, especially **Graff**, and the charming small shops in the Regency **Burlington Arcade**. Almost all of the very central areas have sufficient character to justify just strolling around, but **Covent Garden** should be on most lists, as it boasts outdoor entertainers and a variety of festivals year-round.

With children, this can be a rather tiring area. There are the sights of course – **Trafalgar Square**, recently refurbished, and **Eros** can be added to those already mentioned – and there is also the possibility of a trip to **Hamleys**, the world-famous toy shop. Leaving this aside, the top attractions for families are probably **St James's Park** – which is pretty and interesting enough to provide something for everyone – and **Coram's Fields**, a useful amenity for kids in Bloomsbury.

Suggested walks

To orientate yourself within central London, try one of these three interesting walks below – one 'historical', one 'intellectual' and the third 'cultural'.

"Historical"

The first stroll encompasses London's most impressive historical sights. Begin at Trafalgar Square, making sure to dodge the buses and pigeons (not always in that order). To the west stretches Pall Mall. Stroll down this wide avenue, flanked by impressive gentlemen's clubs, until reaching St James's Palace. (If you get there by 11.15am, you can follow the St James's Palace detachment of the Queen's Guard as it marches to Buckingham Palace – this walk is not short of picture opportunities, as the throngs of tourists will attest.) From Buckingham Palace, one is a short distance from the immaculate St. James's Park – one of the oldest royal parks. Enter on the western edge of the park, walking alongside the lake and passing Duck Island. Exit at the southeast corner and follow Great George Street towards Westminster. The Abbey and the Houses of Parliament will soon come into view. From this point, the final stage of the walk begins. Head north along Parliament Street, which becomes Whitehall, past Downing Street, the Horse Guards and finally back to Trafalgar Square.

"Intellectual"

Our second recommended walk also begins at Trafalgar Square, but heads north, rather than west. Begin by walking up Charing Cross Road. As you pass Leicester Square to your left, and Long Acre to your right, a long literary path unfolds – a book-lover's dream. Along each side of Charing Cross Road until Oxford Street lies almost the full gamut of booksellers – from the niche specialists to the commercial giants – making for an interesting afternoon within the heart of town.

"Cultural"

For a less intellectually strenuous jaunt, begin at Leicester Square and head north along Leicester Place to Lisle Street. Immediately, the colourful restaurants, markets and stores of Chinatown are in full view. Move west to Wardour Street and turn right. Gerrard Street on the right is the pedestrianised centre of Chinatown. Head further north up Wardour Street and you will be thrust into the crowded, teeming streets of Soho. Slowly the area becomes a mix of the chic, the colourful and the exotic. Soho and its environs has something for all tastes, from galleries and gay bars to 'adult' entertainment options and a variety of restaurants. You can move easily in any direction off Wardour Street to explore the secrets of Soho. Perhaps turn left on to Broadwick Street which will lead you to Carnaby Street – the home of swinging '60s London, re-inventing itself once more as a fashion hot-spot after years of being populated with tourist-trap shops. Inevitably, your wanderings will take you to one of the boundaries of Soho – Oxford Street to the north, Regent Street to the west and Charing Cross Road to the east. On all three streets, there are tube stations and bus stops, making a nice end point for your journey.

Indoor attractions

Anaesthesia Museum WC1
www.aagbi.org
21 Portland Pl   (020) 7631 1650   2–1B
The museum is home to one of the largest collections of early and contemporary anaesthetic equipment in the world. Each year a special topic is presented, illustrated with a selection from the 5,000 items in the collection. / Times: Mon-Fri 9.30am-5pm *(appt recommended); Tube: Oxford Circus; Café, Restaurant.*

Architectural Association WC1
www.aaschool.ac.uk
34-36 Bedford Sq
(020) 7887 4000 recorded information (020) 7887 4111
2–1C
For anyone with an interest in architecture, the Association offers a rich and varied programme of afternoon and evening lectures. There are also exhibitions by contemporary architects and students, in the Exhibition Gallery and Photo Library, throughout the year. See the website for further details.
/ Times: Mon-Sat 10am-7pm (Sat 3pm); Tube: Tottenham Court Road; Café, Restaurant, Picnic area (12pm-2pm).

Blewcoat School SW1
www.nationaltrust.org.uk
23 Caxton St   (020) 7222 2877   2–4C
In 1709, local brewer William Green paid for the building of this single room. Its aim was to provide an education for poor children, and it was indeed used as a school until 1926. Bought by the National Trust in 1954, restored in 1975, it is now the Trust's London Gift Shop and Information Centre. / Times: Mon-Fri 10am-5.30pm; Tube: St James's Park.

British Dental Association Museum W1
www.bda.org/museum
64 Wimpole St   (020) 7563 4549   2–1B
A fun visit for all the family! The museum holds around 30,000 items including dental instruments and equipment, furniture, photographs, archives, and art. Highlights include toothache cures, drills and toothpaste advertisements. / Times: Tue and Thu 1pm-4pm; other times by appt ; Tube: Bond Street.

British Museum WCI

www.thebritishmuseum.ac.uk
Great Russell St   (020) 7323 8000   2–1C

Six million visitors a year can't be wrong – this august neo-classical building (Robert Smirke, 1823-52) is London's leading attraction – free or otherwise. It does, after all, house what is arguably the world's greatest collection of antiquities. The museum underwent a series of renovations and redevelopments in preparation for its 250th anniversary, in 2008. The most important of these was the Great Court, which transformed the previously-hidden inner courtyard into one of London's greatest public spaces: a two-acre square, with the great Round Reading Room at its centre, enclosed by a spectacular glass roof.

Particular strengths of the collection include Egyptian antiquities, coins and medals, the collections relating to Greek and Roman civilisation (especially, of course, the marbles from the Parthenon), clocks, and prints and drawings.

No one could possibly take in the whole museum in a day – just to pass by all the exhibits would apparently require a walk of some two and a half miles – so it's probably worth deciding on a section of particular interest and trying to make sense of that. From Mon-Fri, the museum's experts give gallery talks at 1.15pm. Regular 'eyeOpener' tours, lasting approximately 40 minutes, focus on different areas of the museum.

There are many interesting temporary exhibitions (which, excluding the occasional 'blockbuster', are free of charge), regular talks and films, and even occasional art workshops for children. / Times: Sun-Wed 10am-5.30pm, Thu-Fri 10am-8.30pm (selected galleries only); Tube: Russell Square, Tottenham Court Road, Holborn; Café, Restaurant.

British Optical Association Museum WC2

www.college-optometrists.org
42 Craven St   (020) 7766 4353   2–3C

This is the oldest optical museum in the world, founded in 1901, and today holds a collection of over twelve thousand items relating to the history of optometry. / Times: by appt; Tube: Charing Cross.

Burlington Arcade W1

www.burlington-arcade.co.uk
Piccadilly   2–2B

This Regency shopping arcade is perhaps the most timeless place in London for window-shopping. Top-hatted beadles maintain standards – no running, no singing, no carrying large parcels, etc – leaving you in perfect serenity to survey the displays in the windows of the small, elegant shops, some of which still sell hand-made luxury goods. / Times: Mon-Sat 9am-6pm; Tube: Green Park, Piccadilly Circus.

Central London

Canada House SW1
www.unitedkingdom.gc.ca
Trafalgar Sq (entrance at Pall Mall East)　(020) 7258 6421
2–2C
The home of the Canadian High Commission since 1925.
Overlooking Trafalgar Square and heavily renovated in 1998,
the building was originally built by Sir Robert Smirke, who also
designed the British Museum. There are regular themed
exhibitions in the Gallery and Foyer areas, as well as an
Information Centre where visitors can learn more about all
things Canadian. / Times: Mon-Fri 10am-5.30pm; Tube: Charing Cross.

Christie's SW1
www.christies.com
8 King St　(020) 7839 9060　2–3B
The two great international auction-houses (the other, of
course, is Sotheby's, which has its own entry, see also) both
originated in London. Christie's has been helping collectors build
up, and in later generations dispose of, great collections of
pictures and furniture since 1766. Except for the grandest of
sales (to which admission is restricted to those who have
bought catalogues), you are welcome to have a look at the
goods to be auctioned in the days before the sale and, indeed,
to attend the auction itself – one of the best free shows in
town. / Times: Mon-Fri 9am-5pm, Sat and Sun noon-5pm (viewings only);
Tube: Green Park.

City Yeomanry Museum WC2
www.armymuseums.org.uk
10 Stone Buildings, Lincolns Inn　(020) 7405 8112　5–2A
A small museum whose permanent exhibit includes uniforms,
medals and equipment of the Inns of Court Regiment and the
City of London Yeomanry dating from the Napoleonic Wars.
/ Times: by appt only Mon-Fri 10am-4pm; Tube: Chancery Lane.

Contemporary Applied Art W1
www.caa.org.uk
2 Percy St　(020) 7436 2344　2–1C
Britain's largest gallery specialising in contemporary crafts,
including jewellery, fine metalwork, ceramics, wood, textiles,
furniture, glass and paper. Seven exhibitions are held a year –
they are free to attend but, as everything is for sale, your visit
could turn out to be expensive! / Times: Mon-Sat 10am-6pm;
Tube: Goodge Street, Tottenham Court Road.

Courtauld Institute Gallery* WC2
www.courtauld.ac.uk
Somerset House, Strand
(020) 7848 2777, recorded information (020) 7848 2526
2–2D
This world-renowned gallery features a rich collection of works
– from the Renaissance to the c20. Included in the collection is

Manet's Bar at the Folies-Bergères *and* Van Gogh's Self-Portrait with Bandaged Ear. *A visit to the gallery makes a relaxing stop after lunch in nearby Victoria Embankment Gardens. (See also Somerset House) Or you can coincide your visit with one of the free Mon lunchtime talks (1.15pm).* / Times: Mon 10am-2pm (at all times for under 18's, full time UK students and unemployed); Tube: Temple, Covent Garden, Holborn; Café.

Fortnum & Mason W1

www.fortnumandmason.com
181 Piccadilly   (020) 7734 8040   2–2B
The royal grocers (established on this site in 1707) are about as close to a fantasy food shop as you'll ever find. The ground floor, in particular, is a riot of crimson and chandeliers, and the (male) assistants still wear tailcoats. In celebration of its third centenary, the shop has recently been subject to a multi-million pound refurbishment, as part of which the 'circulation' between the floors has been considerably improved, encouraging one to further explore one of the most charming retail interiors in town. The external clock is a well-known landmark – see the outdoor section. / Times: Mon-Sat 10am-8pm, Sun noon-6pm (with browsing time until noon); Tube: Green Park, Piccadilly Circus.

Foyle's WC2

www.foyles.co.uk
113-119 Charing Cross Rd   (020) 7437 5660   2–2C
On its current site for over a century, Foyle's – which, at its height, claimed to be the biggest bookshop in the world – was once seen as a major London institution, an unavoidable stop-off on any provincial's visit to town (whether anything was actually purchased or not). As even the shop concedes, it lost its way in the latter part of the c20, but now – under new management – it's battling back. Indeed, in terms of the books stocked, they claim that this is now the largest bookshop in Europe: its attractions for whiling away an hour or two are self-evident. / Times: Mon-Sat 9.30am-9pm, Sun 11.30am-6pm (with browsing time until noon); Tube: Tottenham Court Road.

Freemasons' Hall WC2

www.grandlodge-england.org
Great Queen St   (020) 7395 9258   2–2D
If you have always been fascinated by the aura of secrecy of Freemasonry, it may come as a surprise that the Masons are very pleased for you to visit their daunting Grand Temple in Covent Garden. The current monolith was dedicated in 1933, but the site has been associated with Freemasonry for over two centuries. The Museum (with collections of porcelain, glassware, jewels, regalia and Masonic memorabilia) are open to the public. For information about tours of the building, visit the website. / Times: Mon-Fri 10am-5pm, Sat by appt; tours Mon-Fri at 11am, 2pm, 3pm and 4pm; Tube: Holborn, Covent Garden.

Getty Images Gallery W1

www.gettyimagesgallery.com
46 Eastcastle St   (020) 7291 5380   2–2C
*London's largest independent photographic gallery, recently
moved from Chelsea. The collections come from the Hulton
Archive which is made up of over 300 collections together
comprising more than 40 million negatives. The gallery also
has frequently changing exhibitions. In the past these have
included "Peacocks and Pinstripes" featuring male fashion
photography, and a "History of the Isle of Man TT Races".*
/ Times: Mon-Fri 10am-6.30pm, Sat noon-6pm; Tube: Oxford Circus.

Grant Museum of Zoology & Comparative Anatomy WC1

www.ucl.ac.uk/museums
University College London, Gower St
(020) 7679 2647   2–1C
*This natural history museum holds some 35,000 specimens
which range right across the animal kingdom, from an
aardvark and gorillas to sloths and a quagga (an extinct type of
zebra) – there are skeletons, specimens in jars and real stuffed
animals. Although it is primarily a resource for education, the
museum is open to anyone by appointment and is popular with
photographers and artists. School groups are also welcome.*
*/ Times: Mon-Fri 1pm-5pm (other times by appt); Tube: Euston, Euston Square,
Warren Street or Goodge Street.*

Grays Antique Market W1

www.egrays.co.uk
58 Davies St   (020) 7629 7034   2–2B
*There are few destinations in London which offer rare gems
and minerals, antique rifles, Islamic art and the River Tyburn
flowing through the basement! These two grand Edwardian
buildings, off Bond Street, are home to an antiques market with
over 200 stalls and shops (including a large antiquarian book
dealer), offering the usual assortment of the useful and useless.
However, the true specialty of the market is the programme of
regular themed exhibitions – subjects vary widely, from Beatles
memorabilia to extensive and ever-popular erotica collections.*
*/ Times: Mon-Wed, Fri 10am-6pm, Thu 10am-8pm, (Sat, Dec only
10am-5pm); Tube: Bond Street.*

Great Ormond Street Hospital for Children WC1

www.gosh.org
Peter Pan Gallery, 55 Great Ormond St
(020) 7405 9200   2–1D
*An exhibition relating to the history of this famous children's
hospital, founded in 1852, is housed in a neighbouring
Georgian town house. Exhibits include photographs and
ephemera. Since 1929, the hospital has received the copyright
proceeds from sales of J M Barrie's Peter Pan (extended in
perpetuity in the UK by a unique Act of Parliament of 1987,
when the copyright expired), and there are letters from the
author (on view by prior request) as well as copies of the book
in a number of languages. / Times: by appt Mon-Fri 9.30am-4.30pm;
Tube: Russell Square, Holborn, Euston.*

Hamleys W1

www.hamleys.co.uk

188 -196 Regent St   (020) 7494 2000   2–2B

At Christmas it may be unbearably crowded, but all year round, this is the number one destination on any child's tour of London – the world's largest toyshop. It has been here for over 125 years. Highlights from the seven jam-packed floors include a large globe on their ground floor, moving displays, a Narnia-themed staircase and a Hornby model railway. / Times: Mon-Fri 10am-8pm, Sat 9am-8pm, Sun noon-6pm; Tube: Piccadilly Circus, Oxford Circus; Café.

Harrods SW1

www.harrods.com

Knightsbridge   (020) 7730 1234   3–1D

Europe's most famous department store works very hard to ensure there is always something new to see in its 25 acres of sales space. First-time visitors should particularly not miss the Food Halls, with their intriguing décor and amazing arrangements of produce, but it is the sheer scale of the whole building and the opulence of some of the goods which are probably the main attractions. Harrods is a little sensitive about its role as a free tourist attraction – the security guards may not admit large parties or people with big bags (or backpacks), dress should be appropriate and photography is not allowed. / Times: Mon-Sat 10am-8pm, Sun 11.30am-6pm; selected food halls open Mon-Sat 9am-9pm, Sun 11.30am-6pm; Tube: Knightsbridge.

Harvey Nichols SW1

www.harveynichols.com

109-125 Knightsbridge   (020) 7235 5000   3–1D

Harvey Nichols is a smaller, more intimate department store than its better-known Knightsbridge neighbour and not, therefore, quite as suited to sightseeing. The particularly innovative window displays are always interesting, though, and the glamorous foodie complex on the fifth floor is worth a look for the sheer improbability of its Dan Dare-style architecture and location. / Times: Mon-Wed 10am-8pm, Thu-Sat 10am-9pm (Fifth Floor Café opens at 8am, Foodmarket opens at 10am), Sun 11.30am-6pm; Tube: Knightsbridge.

Houses of Parliament SW1

www.parliament.uk

(020) 7219 3000   2–3C

No visitor will wish to miss the sight of the Palace of Westminster, with the famous clock tower (whose bell is known as Big Ben). There has been a royal palace here since c11 but, after a disastrous fire in 1835, the building was reconstructed in neo-Gothic style to the designs of Charles Barry and Augustus Pugin.

The building is not generally open to the public, but if you want to see the fine interior – or our ancient democracy at work – there are two ways of going about it. One is to arrange to go on a tour and the other is to watch a debate – in the Commons or Lords (from one of the Strangers' Galleries) or in a Commons committee. Dealing with the former first, UK citizens wishing to have a tour must apply to their MP in writing, and should do so well in advance. Tours of the Palace include the c14 Westminster Hall, where Charles I was tried in 1649. (Tours are usually only available Mon-Wed mornings and Fri afternoons; this varies during parliamentary recesses.)

If you want to watch a debate in progress, the galleries are open to the public. However, priority is given to those with tickets, and the safest course, therefore, to avoid a lengthy queue, is to apply for a ticket, as far in advance as possible, to your MP (or, if you are not a UK citizen, to your embassy or High Commission). Impromptu visitors have a good chance of gaining admission (unless the subject of debate is very controversial) later on in the day – sittings usually go on until 10pm, and sometimes beyond – or on Fri.

If you're planning any visit to Parliament, it's a very good idea to check out your plans with the Public Information Office on the number given. / Tube: Westminster.

Hunterian Museum WC2
www.rcseng.ac.uk
35-43 Lincoln's Inn Fields   (020) 7869 6560   2–1D
The Hunterian Museum collections have been accumulated over 400 years by, among others, surgeon and anatomist John Hunter (1728-1793). The collections consist of human and animal anatomy, wax teaching models, surgical and dental instruments, paintings, drawings and sculpture. The museum has recently undergone extensive refurbishment. There is a curator's tour every Wed at 1pm in addition to regular talks by Museum volunteers covering various aspects of the collections and the history of surgery. / Times: Tue-Sat 10am-5pm; Tube: Holborn, Temple.

Liberty W1
www.liberty.co.uk
214-220 Regent St   (020) 7734 1234   2–2B
Liberty is one of the most charming and individualistic of London's department stores. It occupies very characterful mock-Tudor premises (built in the '20s, from timbers of two men o'war, HMS Impregnable and HMS Hindustan), which are certainly worth a look, especially the creaky staircases. The store's particular strength is house furnishings and it carries many interesting and unusual objects and fabrics, as well as fashions and cosmetics. / Times: Mon-Sat 10am-10pm, Sun noon-6pm; Tube: Oxford Circus; Café, Restaurant.

London Scottish Regimental Museum SW1
www.londonscottishregt.org
95 Horseferry Rd   (020) 7630 1639   2–4C
The collection covers the regiment's uniforms and equipment since its formation in 1859. Exhibits include medals (the regiment has three VCs to its credit), the three war memorials in the Drill Hall, badges, an indexed record of previous members as well as hundreds of photos documenting the history of the Regiment. / Times: by appt Tue-Thu 11am-4pm; Tube: St James's Park.

London Silver Vaults WC2
www.thesilvervaults.com
Chancery House, Chancery Ln   (020) 7242 3844   2–2D
This intriguing, subterranean shopping mall, with its 40 or so silver dealers, claims to offer the largest collection of silverware under one roof in the world. All the items are for sale, with prices ranging from £5 to £500,000, but you're quite welcome just to go and browse. / Times: Mon-Fri 9am-5.30pm, Sat 9am-1pm; Tube: Chancery Lane.

National Gallery WC2
www.nationalgallery.org.uk
Trafalgar Sq   (020) 7747 2885   2–2C
One of the world's great galleries of Western European paintings (some 2300 in number), from the late c13 to the early c20 – Giotto to Picasso. What distinguishes it is the balance of its collection across all of the schools, with practically no great master unrepresented. The Sainsbury Wing (1991) houses the earliest works from 1260 to 1510 (including Botticelli, Bellini and Raphael), and the rest of the collection progresses chronologically through the West Wing (Michelangelo, Holbein, Titian), the North Wing (Rubens, Velázquez, Rembrandt) and the East Wing (Gainsborough, Turner, Constable, Monet, van Gogh), up to 1900. Daily tours of the collection take place (Mon-Sat), at 11.30am and 2.30pm (also Wed at 6.30pm), according to the season, and there are lectures or films about artists or schools of painting at 1pm (daily, Fri 1.15pm). In addition there are family talks on Sun at 10.30am, 11am and 2pm. Every Wed evening, student musicians from the Royal College of Music perform in the Central Hall – for information, pick up a copy of The National Gallery News. If you prefer to let your fingers do the walking (or have a child, of any age, to amuse), don't miss the Micro Gallery Computer Information Room, a great resource for research. There is a charge for some special exhibitions. / Times: Mon-Sun 10am-6pm (Wed 9pm); Tube: Charing Cross, Leicester Square, Embankment; Café, Restaurant.

National Portrait Gallery WC2
www.npg.org.uk
St Martin's Place   (020) 7306 0055,
recorded information (020) 7312 2463   2–2C
This is arguably the most accessible of London's major galleries. Though in most collections it's artistic merit which wins a place, here it's the importance of the subject of the portrait as much

as the eminence of the painter, sculptor or photographer (though many of the great British artists are, of course, represented). Almost all of the major figures of English history are recorded, with the contemporary portraiture galleries being the most popular. The Ondaatje Wing (2000) increased the exhibition space by a half, and includes an IT gallery, lecture theatre, rooftop restaurant (with panoramic city views) and a balcony gallery which specialises in faces from British cultural history. One of the longest escalators in the UK transports visitors up to the top floor, from which they can view the collection chronologically as they return to ground level. Gallery talks, tours and family events are also available – check website for details – and there is music at 6.30pm on Fri. There is a charge for some special exhibitions. / Times: Mon-Sun 10am-6pm (Thu and Fri 9pm); Tube: Leicester Square, Charing Cross; Café, Restaurant.

New London Architecture WC1

www.newlondonarchitecture.org
26 Store St   (020) 7636 4044   1–4C
Want to see what central London looks like at 1:1500 scale? It's difficult to think of a better way of seeing how London all 'fits together' than by a visit to this impressive model. A great starting point for any architectural exploration of the metropolis. / Times: Mon-Fri 9am-6pm, Sat 10am-5pm; Tube: Tottenham Court Rd, Goodge St and Russell Sq; Café.

Petrie Museum of Egyptian Archaeology WC1

www.petrie.ucl.ac.uk
University College, Malet Place   (020) 7679 2884   2–1C
An extraordinary collection of Egyptian antiquities, excavated by the eminent archaeologist Sir Flinders Petrie and his followers since 1884. The collection includes about 80,000 objects, but – pending the opening of a new museum in 2011 – only about 5% are on display. The exhibition is organised to illustrate the development of Egyptian culture from Palaeolithic to Roman and Coptic times. There is also a small Syrian Ptolemaic Roman collection (also excavated by Petrie). / Times: Tue-Fri 1pm-5pm, Sat 11am-2pm; Tube: Warren Street, Goodge Street, Euston Square, Russel Square; Café, Restaurant.

Phillips de Pury & Company SW1

www.phillipsdepury.com
Howick Place   (020) 7318 4023   2–4B
An international contemporary art business which holds both auctions and exhibitions. See the website for forthcoming exhibitions and auctions at its new premises in Westminster. / Times: Mon-Sat 10am-5pm; Tube: St James's Park.

Photographers' Gallery W1

www.photonet.org.uk
16-18 Ramillies St   (0845) 262 1618   2–2C
London's largest public gallery dedicated to photography, recently re-located to a location near Oxford Circus. They've not yet totally realised ambitions for their impressive new building, but the gallery is well worth a visit anyway. / Times: Tue-Sun 11am-6pm (Thu and Fri 8pm); Tube: Oxford Circus; Café.

Poilâne SW1
www.poilane.fr
46 Elizabeth St (020) 7808 4910 3–2D
Bread from the great Parisian bakery, Poilâne, has almost mythical status in the foodie world. At great expense, ovens mimicking those in the rue du Cherche-Midi have been installed in the heart of Belgravia, and you're welcome to stop by to see them in use. Bread-making tends to have finished by the time they open, but you should catch the croissants – if this weren't a book about doing things for free, we'd suggest you bought one for breakfast! / Times: Mon-Fri 7.30am-7pm (Sat 6pm); Tube: Victoria.

RIBA (Royal Institute of British Architects) W1
www.architecture.com
66 Portland Pl (020) 7580 5533 2–1B
The Architecture Centre is an international showcase for the buildings of today and the future, and focuses on awards and competitions. However, it also houses some exhibitions, occasionally on rather eccentric themes. / Times: Mon-Sat 10am-5.30pm (Tue 8pm); Tube: Great Portland Street, Regents Park; Café.

Royal Academy of Arts* W1
www.royalacademy.org.uk
Burlington House, Piccadilly (020) 7300 8000 2–2B
Although there is a charge for all of the exhibitions (of which the most famous is the annual Summer Exhibition), there is no charge for access to the Academy's charming building. In addition, two of its greatest attractions – one architectural, one artistic – are always on view, gratis. The Sackler Galleries extension, built in 1991, is reckoned by many to be one of the most successful modern additions to any period London building (actual entry to the galleries is not free). The glass-sided lift, designed by Lord Foster, by which the galleries are approached, offers a magical journey from the old to the new, and some of the Academy's sculptures are dramatically displayed outside the galleries. At the far end, in its own white space, is displayed the Academy's greatest artistic treasure, the Michelangelo Tondo – the only example in England of the master's sculpture. There are free tours of the early c18 Private Rooms (usually offered three times a week), which are the most characterful part of the Academy – you need to call in advance for details. / Times: Sun-Thu 10am-6pm, Fri 10am-10pm; Tube: Piccadilly Circus, Green Park; Café, Restaurant.

Royal Courts of Justice WC2
www.hmcourts-service.gov.uk
Strand (020) 7947 6000 2–2D
Almost all of the most important civil cases in England and Wales end up being tried in this imposing Victorian Gothic

building. There are usually at least 50 courts sitting at any one time, so you should be able to find something of interest – trials might cover anything from allocating fault for a serious accident to esoteric 'administrative' law cases, in which people can challenge the Government's exercise of its powers. Children under 16 are not admitted. / Times: Mon-Fri 10am-4.30pm; Tube: Temple; Café.

Royal Institution W1
www.rigb.org
21 Albemarle St   (020) 7409 2992   2–2B
Formerly the Faraday Museum, the museum at the recently revamped Royal Institution covers the history of the scientific accomplishments of the RI. The three principal themes are experimentation, people, and communication. Highlights of the collection include Faraday's magnetic laboratory as it was in the 1850s. / Times: Mon-Fri 9am-9pm; Tube: Green Park.

St Martin-in-the-Fields WC2
www.stmartin-in-the-fields.org
Trafalgar Sq   (020) 7839 8362   2–2C
One of the grandest of London's churches – well, its parish does include Buckingham Palace – and a particularly fine sight when floodlit by night. It was designed by James Gibbs and consecrated in 1726, and has recently been subjected to a multi-million pound programme of refurbishment and improvement. There are concerts every weekday (except Wed and Thu) at 1.05pm – a perfect break from one of the most hectic parts of London or a suitable finale to a visit to the neighbouring National Gallery (see also). Wed & Sun, there is a choral evensong at 5pm. Check the website for periodic free events, which includes a Harvest Festival attended by the 'Pearly' Kings and Queens (first Sun in October). / Tube: Charing Cross, Embankment; Café.

Selfridges W1
www.selfridges.co.uk
Oxford St   (0800) 123 400   2–2A
Gordon Selfridge was always a showman, and his great Oxford Street department store – which celebrates its centenary during 2009 – remains true to the spirit of its founder. You don't personally need to be spending tens of thousands on a watch, for example, to be impressed by a stroll through the recently installed Room of Luxury. There's also quite a programme of events throughout the store too – visit the website to see "What's on". / Times: Mon, Tue, Thu-Sat 9.30am-8pm, Wed 9.30am-6pm, Sun noon-6pm; Tube: Bond Street, Marble Arch; Café, Restaurant.

Sir John Soane's Museum WC2
www.soane.org
13 Lincoln's Inn Fields   (020) 7405 2107   2–1D
One of the most extraordinary buildings in the world, consisting of three interconnected townhouses. It was built by the great architect between 1792 and 1824, for his own occupation and as a home for his eclectic collection of treasures. The collection

includes important (and sometimes fascinating) artefacts from Egyptian, Greek and Roman civilisations. There are also some pictures, most famously Hogarth's series of paintings, The Rake's Progress and The Election. The greatest attraction, however, is just wandering around this labyrinthine house, which you may do without any charge (though you do have to pay for conducted tours and some special exhibitions).
/ Times: Tue-Sat 10am-5pm; 1st Tue of month 6pm-9pm; Tube: Holborn.

Somerset House WC2
www.somersethouse.org.uk
Strand   (020) 7845 4600   2–2D
This extraordinary neoclassical palace, by the Thames, is often seen – unadvertised – in TV programmes, as its courtyard in particular is a 'gift' for those seeking period settings. It has also figured in at least two James Bond movies. It's the scale of the place which makes is perhaps the most striking feature of a visit, and especially the central courtyard. Apart from the fountains, which emerge directly from the granite floor, it looks very much as it must have appeared two centuries ago.

On the lower ground floor visitors may watch a (surprisingly) fascinating video which charts the history and many transformations of the building, from a royal palace washed by the River Thames to the office of public bodies such as the Royal Academy and – more recently – the Inland Revenue. An exhibition in the King's Barge House tells the story of the old Tudor palace, which once stood on this site, and features objects recovered during the renovation of the Courtyard. For free guided tours, visit on first and third Sat of each month – check the website for details. / Times: 10am-6pm daily; Tube: Temple; Café, Restaurant, Picnic area.

Sotheby's W1
www.sothebys.com
34-35 New Bond St   (020) 7293 5000   2–2B
Sotheby's is possibly the best known of the great international art auctioneers. Details of access are broadly as for its competitor, Christie's (see also). / Times: Mon-Fri 9am-5pm, occasional weekend viewing (phone to confirm); Tube: Bond Street, Green Park; Café.

Tate Britain SW1
www.tate.org.uk
Millbank
(020) 7887 8000; recorded info (020) 7887 8008   2–4C
This gallery of British art occupies a particularly charming Edwardian building overlooking the Thames at Westminster.

Most British artists of any repute, since 1500, are represented: the Blake and Hogarth collections are particularly fine, and the Clore Galleries house the enormous Turner Bequest.

There are tours of different parts of the collection (lasting about an hour) on weekdays at 11am, noon, 2pm, 3pm, and Sat and Sun at noon and 2pm, as well as weekly lectures and films.

The website includes a daily calendar, which specifically flags free events. (The Tate's international modern art collection now resides at Tate Modern, see South.) / Times: Mon-Sun 10am-5.50pm (1st Fri of each month 10am-10pm); Tube: Pimlico; Café.

Twinings WC2
www.twinings.co.uk
216 Strand   (020) 7353 3511   2–2D
Dating from 1706, the shop of the famous tea company claims to be the oldest in London in its original ownership, and still selling the same product. It certainly has a lot of period charm and its compact premises (suitable for small parties only) house a collection illustrating the history of Twinings and its involvement in tea. / Times: Mon-Fri 9am-5pm, Sat 10am-4pm; Tube: Temple.

UCL: Art Collections WC1
www.ucl.ac.uk/museums
University College London, Gower St
(020) 7679 2540   2–1C
John Flaxman (1755-1826) was a pre-eminent name in the emergence of neo-classicism in England and, in 1810, he became the first Professor of Sculpture at the Royal Academy. Plaster models from which his marble sculptures were subsequently made are on permanent display in the Flaxman Gallery. In the Strang Print Room there is a display, changing each term, drawn from the College Art Collections – a diverse assemblage of over 10,000 items dating from 1490 (and including works from Constable, Turner, Durer, Rembrandt and van Dyck as well as early Slade School work from famous artists). Free events and workshops throughout the year – check website for details. / Times: Flaxman and Strang Print Room Mon-Fri 1pm-5pm (other times by appt); Tube: Warren Street, Goodge Street.

UCL: Ethnographic Collections WC1
www.ucl.ac.uk/museums
University College London, Gower St
(020) 7679 1038   2–1C
The collections contain various objects from all over the world having to do with Material Culture, such as textiles and other artefacts. Many of the items were acquired by Daryll Forde, the founder of the Department of Anthropology at UCL. / Times: by appt; Tube: Goodge Street, Euston Square.

UCL: Galton Collection WCI

www.ucl.ac.uk/museums
University College London, Gower St
(020) 7679 2457   2–IC

A collection made up of 500 scientific instruments, papers, and personal memorabilia belonging to Sir Francis Galton (1822-1911). Highlights of the collection include craniometers, glass eyes, hair samples, fingerprinting kits, and map plates for the first weather charts of Britain, which were published in the Times. / Times: by appt; Tube: Goodge Street, Euston Square.

UCL: Geology Collections WCI

www.ucl.ac.uk/museums
University College London, Gower St
(020) 7679 7900   2–IC

Rocks, fossils and minerals collected from all over the world. Highlights include the Johnston-Lavis volcanological collection and the UK repository for NASA images and maps. / Times: Rock Room Wed noon-2pm, Planetary Centre third Wed of the month noon-1pm, other collections by appt; Tube: Goodge Street, Euston Square.

UCL: Institute of Archaeology Collections WCI

www.ucl.ac.uk/museums
University College London, Gower St
(020) 7679 4789   2–IC

Important archaeological items from all over the world. Items include Classical Greek and Roman ceramics and material excavated from Jericho by Kathleen Kenyon. / Times: foyer Mon-Fri 9am-5pm, Collections by appt; Tube: Goodge Street, Euston Square.

UCL: Science Collections WCI

www.ucl.ac.uk/museums
University College London, Gower St
(020) 7679 1038   2–IC

The collections at UCL contain scientific equipment and memorabilia used by various UCL scientists over the last 200 years. Topics include chemistry, physiology, physics, and engineering. / Times: by appt; Tube: Goodge Street, Euston Square.

Wallace Collection WI

www.wallacecollection.org
Manchester Sq   (020) 7563 9500   2–IA

Hertford House, an imposing and sumptuous mansion just north of Oxford Street, contains one of the most splendid collections of pictures and artefacts in London, bequeathed to the nation by Lady Wallace in 1897. It has been suggested that one of the galleries, with its pictures by Watteau and Fragonard, houses the finest group of French c18 pictures which can be seen in a single room anywhere. The collection also includes works by Rembrandt, Rubens and Hals (Laughing Cavalier). Extraordinary clocks, Sèvres porcelain and armour are among the other attractions. Free general guided tours are conducted at 1pm on weekdays (also at 11.30am Wed and Sat and 3pm Sun). / Times: Mon-Sun 10am-5pm; Tube: Bond Street; Café, Restaurant.

Westminster Abbey* SW1
www.westminster-abbey.org
(020) 7222 5152   2–3C
Sadly, in reaction to sheer force of numbers (over 3 million visitors a year), no part of the interior of this great and historic church – whose consecration predated the 1066 Invasion – is now open gratis to the public. You can always attend a service of course – the choir has a fine reputation – or, if your taste is for something more secular, there is a short weekly organ recital at 5.45pm on Sun. Such visits, however, will provide very limited opportunities to explore the architecture and the many monuments to famous folk.

You can, however, visit the cloisters, which – opening off the quiet garden square behind the abbey – are one of the most atmospheric parts. Rebuilt after a fire in 1298, they would in fact once have been the busiest parts of the Abbey. One can traverse the cloisters to visit the College Garden (donations appreciated), where the Abbey's first Infirmary garden was established in the c11. During July and August, bands play there on Thu between 12.30pm-2pm. / Tube: Westminster, St James's Park.

Westminster Cathedral SW1
www.westminstercathedral.org.uk
Victoria St   (020) 7798 9055   2–4C
Completed in 1903, this Byzantine-style Roman Catholic cathedral houses some fine marble work and mosaics, with the sculptures of the 14 Stations of the Cross by Eric Gill being particularly renowned. It is famous for its choir, and services are sung daily except in August. Unfortunately there is a small charge to ascend the campanile (bell tower), which gives a fine view over much of London. / Times: Mon-Sun 7am (Sat 8am)-7pm; Tube: Victoria.

Westminster City Archives SW1
www.westminster.gov.uk
10 St Ann's St   (020) 7641 6000   2–4C
Most boroughs have an archive, and if you are at all interested in the history of a particular area, make sure to check it out. These can be quite fascinating places, filled with information on all aspects of local life you might never otherwise have considered looking for, and family historians find them a particularly helpful resource. In addition, there are usually exhibitions on aspects of local history. This being Westminster, these particular archives are very extensive. They are housed in an impressive building, tucked away behind the Abbey. Over 5 kilometres of shelving hold around 60,000 items – the earliest is dated 1256. / Times: Tue-Thu 10am-7pm, Fri-Sat 10am-5pm; Tube: St James's Park.

Outdoor attractions

Berwick Street Market W1
Berwick St   2–2C
It's the characterful, seedy location that is the main attraction of this atmospheric, small street market situated amongst record shops, fabric warehouses and vice dens in Soho. It specialises in cheap fruit and veg and there are also some decent fish, bread and cheese stalls as well as others selling general household goods. / Times: Mon-Sat 9am-5pm; Tube: Piccadilly Circus.

Buckingham Palace* SW1
www.royal.gov.uk
(020) 7930 4832   2–3B
This house has been the principal residence of the Sovereign only since Victoria's day. You know if Her Majesty is at home because the royal standard (a red, gold and blue quartered flag, with lions and a harp) replaces the Union Flag on the flagpole. (You will also note four guards on duty, instead of the two who suffice at other times.) The main façade, facing the Mall, is much more recent (1913) than the rest of the building and, as is often noted, gives the impression of nothing so much as a more-important-than-usual branch of Barclays Bank. To get a better (and more sympathetic) feeling of what lies behind the façade, walk down Buckingham Gate, and appreciate the side view of the palace. The Queen's private quarters are on the other side, overlooking Constitution Hill. (There is a charge for the summer tours of the gardens, and the interior of the palace, as there is for admission to the Queen's Gallery or the Royal Mews.) One of the most opportune times to visit, of course, is for the Changing of the Guard (see also). / Tube: St James's Park, Victoria, Green Park.

Cleopatra's Needle WC2
Victoria Embankment   2–2D
This 3,500-year-old obelisk, weighing about 186 tons, now by the side of the Thames, was taken from near the Temple of the Sun God in Heliopolis in Egypt. It was presented to Britain by the Turkish Viceroy in 1819 and has a twin, which stands in New York's Central Park. The two lions which 'guard' the needle were incorrectly placed (they should actually face away, to keep watch), but their position has never been corrected. / Tube: Embankment.

Coram's Fields WC1
www.coramsfields.org
93 Guilford St   (020) 7837 6138   2–1D
Seven acres of central London to which adults (over 16) are not admitted – unless accompanied by a child! This shaded

*playground – the legacy of an c18 philanthropist – is a boon
for harassed parents. It boasts play equipment, a sports area,
paddling pool, pets corner and a duck pond. On your way
home, you might like to 'tick off' the house in which Charles
Dickens lived, nearby, at 48 Doughty Street.* / Times: summer
9am-7pm, winter 9am-dusk; Tube: Russell Square; Café, Restaurant, Picnic area
(open School holidays only).

Covent Garden WC2
www.coventgardenlondonuk.com
The Market   (020) 7836 9136   2–2C
*Site of the main wholesale fruit 'n' veg market of the
metropolis until the '70s, Covent Garden is now a major tourist
hang-out. With its c18 market setting and its colourful shops,
stalls and cafés, it is certainly one of the most agreeable and
popular places for a stroll in central London, if arguably a
victim of its own popularity. On the positive side, there's almost
invariably something going on in the way of musical
performances, busking or more serious street-theatre. There is
a reason for that – this is private property, and only 'selected'
performers are allowed. (You can get further information about
them on the website.)*

*Just north of Covent Garden lies Neal Street. This was formerly
a warehouse district, but now is refurbished, with some
eccentric stores, and regular street performers.* / Tube: Covent
Garden, Leicester Square; Café.

Eros SW1
Piccadilly Circus   2–2C
*Although invariably known as Eros, the famous, small statue at
Piccadilly Circus in fact represents the Angel of Christian
Charity. Unveiled in 1893, it was London's first statue to be
made of aluminium, at the time a rare and unusual material,
and commemorates the philanthropist Lord Shaftesbury (whose
Avenue is nearby).* / Tube: Piccadilly Circus.

Fortnum & Mason Clock W1
www.fortnumandmason.co .uk
181 Piccadilly   (020) 7734 8040   2–2B
*On the hour, every hour, four-foot-high figures of Mr Fortnum
and Mr Mason – the c18 palace servants who went on to
establish the famous grocers – emerge from doors above their
shop's main entrance, face each other and bow. A c18 air is
then played on 17 bells. The two gentlemen then bow again
and retire to their respective quarters. All-in-all, it's quite an
amusing performance from what would now seem to be central
London's only performing clock.* / Tube: Piccadilly Circus, Green Park.

Graff W1
www.graffdiamonds.com
6-7 New Bond St   (020) 7584 8571   2–2B
If you're only going to look at one shop window in London, it should probably be the armour-glazed display which – literally – bedazzles shoppers who stand outside this Mayfair jeweller. Graff is the world's leading dealer in rare coloured diamonds, and the shop window always displays a fascinating and beautiful range of implausibly large sparklers. / Times: Mon-Fri 9.30am-5.30pm; Tube: Green Park.

Green Park SW1
www.royalparks.gov.uk
(020) 7930 1793   2–3B
The park was originally meadowland used for hunting, and duels were regularly fought here until the mid-c17. Now the 53 acres by Piccadilly comprise what the unkind might describe as the Ugly Duckling of the Royal Parks – alone among them, it lacks a lake, flowers, summer music and a café. It is, however, a relaxing place and very central. Constitution Hill (which runs along the park's southern border) is so-called in commemoration of Charles II's morning walks. / Times: 24 hours; Tube: Green Park, Hyde Park Corner; Café, Picnic area.

Old Bond Street W1
2–2B
If you're seriously into window-shopping, you certainly shouldn't miss the extraordinary row of shops to be found in this street which, for more than three centuries, has been London's most fashionable boutique thoroughfare – and which has enjoyed renewed popularity in recent years. In particular, check out the cluster – or should that be lustre? – of the world's greatest jewellers, clustered around the junction with Burlington Gardens. The place Vendôme and Fifth Avenue may trump Bond Street for scale, but if you're looking for a concentration of starry names in a small space, nowhere else comes close. Note especially the window of Graff – see separate entry. / Tube: Green Park.

Riverside Walk
www.visitthames.co.uk
See the introduction of the South section for suggestions of interesting walks by the Thames.

Roman Bath WC2

www.nationaltrust.org.uk

5 Strand Ln   (020) 8232 5050   2–2D

A whodunnit (or rather 'who built it') mystery surrounds the remains of a bath restored in the c17 and believed by some people to be Roman. It's more in the nature of a curiosity than a serious attraction, and if you find your way there, you can see 90 per cent of what there is to see through the window. Peer in, read the printed notice and decide the origins for yourself. If you're determined to have a proper investigation, though, you can call the number given to arrange an appointment to view. / Times: Wed 1pm-5pm by appt (1 Apr-30 Sep); Tube: Temple (not Sun), Blackfriars, Charing Cross.

St James's Park SW1

www.royalparks.gov.uk

(020) 7930 1793   2–3C

This is possibly the most beautiful, and certainly the most highly cultivated, of the Royal Parks. Situated in the ceremonial heart of London, between Westminster and Buckingham Palace, it offers idyllic views in both directions. The park (93 acres in extent) was acquired by Henry VIII as a deer park for St James's Palace, but owes much of its current appearance to John Nash, whose designs were commissioned in the reign of George IV. During the summer, there are frequent weekend concerts at the bandstand, and gun salutes (see also) on ceremonial occasions. The pelicans are fed from 2.30pm-3pm daily, by Duck Island. / Times: 5am-midnight; Tube: St James's Park; Café.

Trafalgar Square WC2

www.london.gov.uk

2–2C

This great central square, dominated by the National Gallery (see also), is famous for its 170-foot high column dedicated to the memory of Lord Nelson (1843), its fountains and its pigeons. It's been refurbished and partially pedestrianised in recent years, and the steps in front of the Gallery have become some sort of answer to Rome's Spanish Steps – a place where (generally younger) people gather on warm evenings to watch the sun go down (over the Palace of Westminster). The statues of imperial lions (Landseer, 1867) remain one of its most popular features (despite the fact that real lions never sit as represented – they always lie on their side). / Tube: Leicester Square, Charing Cross; Café.

Victoria Embankment Gardens WC2

Villiers St   (020) 7641 5263   2–2D

This colourful, elongated park lies a few short steps from the traffic and bustle of the Strand. Spring and summer usher in not only a profusion of blooms but also an array of entertainments, such as dance, mime, music, poetry and opera festivals. In spite of its attraction and especially considering the major road running alongside, it is surprisingly peaceful. An ideal spot to lunch – nearby Villiers Street has a plethora of sandwich shops — it's very popular with local office workers. York Watergate (1626) is an attractive curiosity, and there are many plaques and explanatory notices about the history of the area to educate you. The largest of these reminds you that, until the construction of the Embankment in 1828, all of what is today the gardens was submerged beneath the Thames! / Times: 7.30-dusk; Tube: Charing Cross, Embankment; Café.

Victoria Tower Gardens SW1
Millbank   2–4D
This quiet and extremely scenic garden, beneath the looming presence of the Victoria Tower (at the other end of the Houses of Parliament from Big Ben) is graced by a cast of Rodin's Six Burghers of Calais and a bronze of the Suffragette, Emmeline Pankhurst, More practically, there is also a children's play area. / Times: 7am-dusk; Tube: Westminster.

Wellington Arch* W1
www.english-heritage.org.uk
Hyde Park Corner   (020) 7930 2726   2–3A
The Wellington Arch bears the largest piece of sculpture in London, Quadriga, by Adrian Jones (1912), in which a figure of Peace descends upon the Chariot of War. The neo-classical Arch itself was built to celebrate the Duke of Wellington's victories over Napoleon, and was completed in 1828, originally bearing a gigantic statue of the Iron Duke himself. Before restoration by English Heritage in 1999, the arch contained London's smallest police station. Colourful illuminations make night-time visits the most rewarding. / Times: Wed-Sun 10am-5pm (1 Nov-31 Mar 4pm); Tube: Hyde Park Corner.

West London

Introduction

West London offers a lot of possibilities to those who want to combine a little artistic or intellectual interest (perhaps a trip to the **Victoria & Albert Museum** or the **Serpentine Gallery**) with a visit to one of the beautiful parks which dot the area, such as **Hyde Park**, **Kensington Gardens** or **Holland Park**.

This combination makes it an excellent area for days out with children, for whom the **Natural History Museum** and **Science Museum** are top attractions.

Away from the centre and its famous parks, the area is rich with fine houses and gardens, such as **Osterley Park** and **Chiswick House**. Take a picnic, and both places should, if the weather is fine, provide a good day out. Both houses are convenient for a riverside walk, either for a stroll after lunch or for some more serious exercise. For those who prefer to amble in a more urban environment, the pleasures of Saturday's **Portobello Road market** are hard to beat.

Some lesser-known attractions well worth investigating include the **Royal Hospital** (and the neighbouring **Ranelagh Gardens**) in Chelsea and **Kensington Roof Gardens** in, yes, Kensington. Further out, **Pitzhanger Manor House** and **Gunnersbury Park Museum** offer interesting and attractive houses to visit, set in pleasant parks.

Hillingdon Tourist Information Centre
www.hillingdon.gov.uk
Uxbridge Central Library, High St, Uxbridge
(01895) 250706
The TIC and library keep the same hours. / Times: Mon, Tue and Thu 9.30am-8pm, Wed and Fri 9.30am-5.30pm, Sat 9.30-4pm), Sun 12.30pm-4.30pm; Tube: Uxbridge.

Twickenham Tourism Information Centre
www.visitrichmond.co.uk
Civic Centre, 44 York St   (020) 8891 7272
/ Times: Mon-Thu 9am-5.15pm (5pm Fri); BR: Twickenham.

Suggested walk

A casual walk in this section of London can lead you through elegant shopping and some charming residential streets. Begin at Sloane Square and head north along Sloane Street with its ever more impressive selection of 'designer' stores. Turn left up Pont Street to Beauchamp Place, famous for its chi-chi shops and 'village' atmosphere. Keep going and you're on Brompton Road – turn right and quickly the massive shopping icon of Harrods looms.

Continue east along the Brompton Road, perhaps, stopping to look at the vast new apartment building overlooking Hyde Park, which is reported to include some of the world's most valuable flats. At the end of Brompton Road, cross Knightsbridge to enter Hyde Park – an ideal spot for a picnic. In the park, stroll along the Serpentine, perhaps, checking out the latest contemporary art show at the Serpentine Gallery.

Indoor attractions

Bonhams SW7
www.bonhams.com
Montpelier St   (020) 7393 3900   3–1C
If you're in the market for a fine and rare cased self-opening 20-bore Royal Brevis side-lock ejector sporting gun by Holland & Holland or a brilliant-cut diamond heart-shaped pendant – or, as a reader of this book just want a look at such items – Bonhams art auctions may be the place for you. / Times: Mon-Fri 9am-5pm; Tube: Knightsbridge.

Boston Manor House
www.fobm.org.uk
Boston Manor Rd, Brentford
(020) 8560 5441, (0845) 456 2800
This Jacobean manor house was built in 1623 and extended in 1670, when it was bought by the Clitherow family, whose home it remained until 1924. The first floor State Rooms have English Renaissance plaster ceilings and impressive historic furniture. The drawing room ceiling of 1623 has panels representing the five senses, the four elements, War and Peace, Peace and Plenty, and Faith, Hope and Charity. The early c19 ground floor rooms house paintings relating to the locality. / Times: Sat, Sun and bank hols 2.30pm-5pm, from 1st Sat in Apr to last Sun in Oct; Tube: Boston Manor.

Brompton Oratory SW7

www.bromptonoratory.com
Thurloe Place, Brompton Rd   (020) 7808 0900   3–2C
Popularly but incorrectly known as the 'Brompton Oratory' (real name: Church of the Immaculate Heart of Mary), this imposing South Kensington landmark is the second largest Catholic church in London, with a nave exceeding in width even that of St Paul's Cathedral. Built in a neo-baroque style, it was constructed between 1880-1884 by Cardinal Newman – one of the great religious figures and thinkers of the c19. Its choir has something of a reputation, and there are three choral services a week as well as during holy festivals. Mass is still said in Latin on Sun and during Easter. / Times: 8am-6pm daily; Tube: South Kensington.

Chelsea Antiques Market SW3

245-253 Kings Rd   3–3C
If you love nothing more than browsing among bric-a-brac and antiques, this is the place for you. In the heart of Chelsea, this characterful arcade is packed with stalls brimming with all sorts of collectables, including books and jewellery in a wide variety of styles. / Times: Mon-Sat 10am-6pm; Tube, Bus: Sloane Square.

Fulham Palace & Gallery SW6

www.fulhampalace.org
Bishop's Avenue   (020) 7736 8140   1–4B
Fulham Palace was the country home of the Bishops of London from the c11 until 1975. There is now a museum telling its long history and a gallery offering a programme of contemporary art. / Times: Mon, Tue noon-4pm, Sat 11am-2pm, Sun 11.30am-3.30pm; Tube: Putney Bridge; Restaurant.

Goethe Institut SW7

www.goethe.de/london
50 Princes Gate, Exhibition Rd   (020) 7596 4000   3–1C
The Institute's task is "to promote the German language and to foster international cultural co-operation", to which end it organises various events relating to German culture. There is a small gallery which has changing exhibitions of works in some way connected with the country. Small parties (one or two people) can pre-book to view a video from the extensive collection, which includes documentaries and dramas. / Times: Mon-Thu noon-8pm, Sat 11am-5pm; Tube: South Kensington; Café, Restaurant.

Gunnersbury Park Museum W3

www.ealing.gov.uk
Gunnersbury Park, Popes Ln   (020) 8992 1612   1–3A
A very grand local museum, housing a large collection on the history of Ealing and Hounslow, but also temporary exhibitions on wider themes – not always of purely local interest – and there are occasional talks relating to the collections. Housed in a former Rothschild family house, built in 1835 on the site of a former royal residence, it benefits from an extremely pleasant park location. On summer weekends you can visit the original Victorian kitchens. / Times: Mon-Sun 11am-5pm (Oct-Mar 4pm); Tube: Acton Town; Café (open summer only).

Hillingdon Local Studies Archives and Museums Service, Middx

www.hillingdon.gov.uk
Uxbridge Central Library, High St, Uxbridge
(01895) 250702
A small museum with historical items relating to the area, the local studies exhibits are generally open to view; archives and museum content can be viewed by appointment. The archives range in date from the c12 to the 1990s. / Times: Mon 9.30am-8pm, Tue-Thu 1pm-5.30 pm, Fri 10am-12.30pm and 1.30 pm-5.30 pm, Sat 9.30am-noon and 1pm-4pm; Tube: Uxbridge.

Hogarth's House W4

Hogarth Ln, Great West Rd   (020) 8994 6757   1–3A
The Chiswick home of the great English engraver and painter William Hogarth (1697-1764) was restored in 1997 to celebrate the tercentenary of his birth. It contains memorabilia of his life, work and circle. The main attractions, however, are his most famous series of engravings (such as Marriage à la Mode and the Rake's Progress) and the attractive garden, which contains a mulberry tree dating from the painter's time. / Times: Tue-Fri 1pm-5pm, Sat-Sun 1pm-6pm (1 Nov-31 Mar Tues-Fri 4pm, Sat-Sun 5pm), closed Jan; Tube: Turnham Green.

Leighton House Museum & Art Gallery W14

www.rbkc.gov.uk
12 Holland Park Rd   (020) 7602 3316   1–3B
An extraordinary mid-Victorian house, with later Moorish Hall (complete with small pool), which provides an evocative setting for the permanent collection of paintings by Frederic, Lord Leighton (1830-96) and some of his contemporaries. NB The house will be closed for a major refurbishment for almost all of 2009. / Times: Wed-Mon 11am-5.30pm; Tube: High Street Kensington.

Narwhal Inuit Art Gallery W4

www.narwhalgallery.com
55 Linden Gardens   (020) 8742 1268   1–3A
A gallery with an unusual theme – Inuit (Eskimo) art of Canada, Russia, Alaska and Greenland. The culture dates back 15,000 years, and, even though there is no Inuit word for 'art', the collection includes sculptures, prints, wall hangings, ceramics, woven baskets, embroidery, carvings and graphics. View by prior appointment only. / Tube: Turnham Green.

National Army Museum SW3

www.national-army-museum.ac.uk
Royal Hospital Rd   (020) 7730 0717   3–3D
The Army's own museum relates its history, from the archers of Henry V to involvement in contemporary UN peacekeeping operations. The emphasis is on the story of the individual soldier – the "human aspect". There is a major collection of

uniforms, life-sized models in costumes through the ages, paintings of famous battle scenes, portraits by Reynolds and Gainsborough and displays of weaponry and medals, as well as some interactive aspects – visitors are welcome to try on helmets and play with the dioramas. A visit here makes a good fit with a trip to the neighbouring Royal Hospital (see also).
/ Times: 10am-5.30pm daily; Tube: Sloane Square.

Natural History Museum SW7
www.nhm.ac.uk
Cromwell Rd   (020) 7942 5000   3–2C
A huge and impressive South Kensington museum offering an incredible amount to see, with exhibits drawn from a collection of 70 million plants, animals, fossils, rocks and minerals. Highlights of the museum include the Aurora Pyramid of Hope, a collection of 296 naturally coloured diamonds and the Dinosaurs gallery which features a fearsome, robotic Tyrannosaurus rex, who not only moves and roars, but also smells realistic! The museum has many interactive displays, and the Investigate Centre offers a hands-on education space where you can examine hundreds of real natural history specimens.
/ Times: 10am-5.50pm, Sun 11am-5.50pm; Tube: South Kensington; Café, Restaurant, Picnic area.

Orleans House Gallery, Middx
www.richmond.gov.uk
Riverside, Twickenham   (020) 8831 6000
Twickenham benefits from an unusually attractive gallery in which to display its borough art collection and to hold contemporary art exhibitions (around six annually). It was designed by James Gibbs in 1720, as the garden pavilion of a very grand house (itself demolished two centuries later) and is richly decorated with ornamental mouldings and gilt. The setting, in a picturesque woodland garden by the Thames (open daylight hours), is a good place for a picnic or as a starting point for a stroll along the river. During the summer (Apr-Oct), one can also visit the Stables Gallery, which holds frequently-changing exhibitions. / Times: Tue-Sat 1pm-5.30pm (Oct-Mar 4.30pm), Sun and bank hols 2pm-5.30pm (Oct-Mar 4.30pm); Tube: Richmond or BR: St Margarets (closer than tube); Café, Picnic area.

Pitzhanger Manor House W5
www.ealing.gov.uk
Mattock Ln   (020) 8567 1227   1–3A
This Ealing house, set in a park, already had the benefit of some exquisite plaster work designed by George Dance in the mid-c18 when it attracted the attentions of the great neo-classical architect Sir John Soane. Between 1800 and 1810, he transformed the house into a Regency villa for himself and his family. The building (Grade I listed) merits a visit in its own right. The house is also home to the Hull Grundy Bequest, the largest public collection of Martinware – the Victorian art

pottery made by the four Martin brothers of Southall between 1877 and 1923 – in the country. The brothers were best known for their bird sculptures and bowls, vessels adorned with sea creatures, and tiles, designed in a capricious but highly-skilled style. There's also an art gallery with changing exhibitions of contemporary art. / Times: Tue-Fri 1pm-5pm, Sat 11am-5pm (Apr-Sep open Sun 1pm-5pm); Tube: Ealing Broadway.

Polish Institute & Sikorsi Museum SW7

www.sikorskimuseum.co.uk
20 Princes Gate   (020) 7589 9249   3–1C
Anyone with even a passing interest in Poland or in military history should visit this elegant museum near Hyde Park – it is by far the most important collection of Polish material anywhere outside that country. There are important mementoes of the many conflicts in which Poles have been involved – including the national flag flown over the ruins of the monastery of Monte Cassino in 1944. The archives contain around two million documents, as well as other materials from the Polish Government and Polish Embassies around the world, mostly from WWII (when they came to London, rather than to the Communist Government in Poland). A photograph and film archive is also available for viewing. / Times: Tue-Fri 2pm-4pm; 1st Sat of month 10am-4pm; archives Tue-Fri 9.30am-4pm; Tube: South Kensington, Knightsbridge.

Royal College of Art SW7

www.rca.ac.uk
Kensington Gore   (020) 7590 4444   3–1B
This is the only exclusively post-graduate university of art and design in the world – famous graduates include David Hockney, Henry Moore and Barbara Hepworth. Courses range from painting, through fashion, to vehicle design and curating. There's almost always an exhibition in progress and most are free – check the website for details. / Times: Mon-Fri 10am-6pm (hours can vary by exhibition, call ahead); Tube: Knightsbridge, South Kensington, High Street Kensington.

Royal College of Music – Department of Portraits & Performance History SW7

www.rcm.ac.uk
Prince Consort Rd   (020) 7591 4340   3–1B
A collection of over 800 instruments from around 1480 to the present, including items from Europe, Asia and Africa. The museum also displays paintings from the RCM's collection. / Times: Portrait Collection, when in operation, Mon-Fri 10am-5.30pm by telephone appt; Museum Wed 2pm-4.30pm during term time, except Jan; Tube: South Kensington, Gloucester Road.

Royal Hospital Chelsea SW3
www.chelsea-pensioners.org.uk
Royal Hospital Rd   (020) 7730 5282   3–3D
Wren's elegant 1682 building, founded by Charles II for veteran soldiers, is still the home of the Chelsea Pensioners, who can sometimes be spotted around the area wearing their splendid scarlet uniforms. Areas you can visit include the Great Hall, the Chapel and the Museum. Don't miss the lovely grounds, Ranelagh Gardens (see also). / Times: Mon-Fri 10am-noon and 2pm-4pm; Tube: Sloane Square; Café, Restaurant, Picnic area.

Saatchi Gallery SW3
www.saatchi-gallery.co.uk
Duke of York's HQ, King's Rd   (020) 7823 2332   3–3D
The Saatchi Gallery – a personal project of the eponymous advertising moghul and famous collector of modern art – recently opened in the Duke of York's HQ on King's Road in Chelsea, in a building of 70,000 square feet. The gallery opened with an exhibition of painting, sculpture and installations by 24 of China's leading artists. There is free admission to all shows – including temporary exhibitions. / Times: 10am-6pm daily; Tube: Sloane Square.

Science Museum SW7
www.sciencemuseum.org.uk
Exhibition Rd   (0870) 870 4771   3–1C
Appropriately for the prime technological museum of the first industrial nation, the 200,000 exhibits of the Science Museum contain many 'firsts' – the first steam engine of the c18 and the first steam turbine of the c19, Stephenson's train (the Rocket) and the Vickers Vimy aircraft which made the first non-stop Atlantic crossing in 1919. Many attractions are more recent, including the Apollo 10 spacecraft, scorched from re-entry into the atmosphere. There's always a great deal going on throughout the museum, and there are enough 'hands-on' exhibits in the 40 galleries to keep children from as young as three happy. Six new interactive galleries, ranging from digital technology to genetics, were recently added. There are charges for some special exhibitions. / Times: 10am-6pm daily; Tube: South Kensington; Café.

Serpentine Gallery W2
www.serpentinegallery.org
Kensington Gardens   (020) 7298 1515 info line   3–1C
An attractive and popular Hyde Park gallery which was remodelled at huge expense in the late-'80s... to ensure that it looked for all the world like the inter-war teahouse it originally was! It stages a number of modern and contemporary exhibitions annually of artists from around the globe. There are usually talks by artists and critics on Sat afternoons at 3pm. / Times: 10am-6pm daily; Tube: Lancaster Gate, South Kensington; Café.

Victoria & Albert Museum SW7

www.vam.ac.uk

Cromwell Rd (0870) 442 0808, (020) 7942 2000 3–2C

Founded in 1852, the "world's largest decorative arts and design museum" comprises over 145 galleries, reflecting centuries of artistic achievement from Europe, the Far East, South East Asia and the Islamic world. There are extensive collections of ceramics, furniture, jewellery and dress, from ancient times to the present day. The British Galleries comprise fifteen galleries dedicated to British design and decorative art from 1500-1900. Other star attractions include a collection of Raphael's seven tapestry cartoons – preparatory designs for tapestries – depicting the acts of Christ's apostles. The cartoons, claimed among the greatest artistic treasures in Britain, were originally commissioned by Pope Leo XI for the Sistine Chapel. Charge for some special exhibitions.
/ Times: Mon-Sun 10am-5.45pm (Wed and last Fri of the month 10pm); Tube: South Kensington; Café, Restaurant.

William Morris Society W6

www.morrissociety.org

Kelmscott House, 26 Upper Mall (020) 8741 3735 1–3A

Occupying part of the house in which Morris – socialist, designer and author – lived from 1878 until his death in 1896, this small collection of memorabilia, designs and books includes one of the original presses on which his novels, poetry and pamphlets were printed. (Devotees should also see the entry for the William Morris Gallery in the East End section.)
/ Times: Thu and Sat 2pm-5pm; Tube: Ravenscourt Park.

Outdoor attractions

Albert Memorial SW7

www.royalparks.org.uk

Prince's Gate, Kensington Gore 3–1B

The Albert Memorial was conceived in 1852, to commemorate the Great Exhibition (the Crystal Palace having already been dismantled, and removed from Hyde Park). It was always intended that it would feature a statue of Victoria's consort, Prince Albert, but his death in 1861 (years before completion of the monument) changed the focus to the man himself. The memorial is a riotous monument to a certain type of Victorian taste, and is decorated with nearly 200 statues representing the arts, sciences, industries, continents and moral virtues, while the frieze of Parnassus depicts 169 life-size figures of the world's artistic genii. / Tube: Knightsbridge, South Kensington.

Bayswater Road Market W2

Bayswater Rd 1–2B

Wander along the north edge of Kensington Gardens on a Sun afternoon, and seemingly every piece of railing is covered with temporary pitches of artists hawking their wares. Amongst the cheesy canvasses designed to woo dewy-eyed tourists you can find some surprisingly good pieces of work – as well as paintings and sketches, there are also generally sculptures and handmade jewellery. / Times: Sun 10am-6pm; Tube, Bus: Lancaster Gate, Queensway.

Brent Lodge Park W7

www.ealing.gov.uk

Church Rd, Hanwell   (020) 8566 1929   1–2A

Once known as 'the bunny park' because of its teeming rabbit population, this expansive area – some 800 acres – has wide open spaces surrounded by dense pockets of trees, and makes a good destination for a quiet picnic or a family day out. The river Brent crosses directly through the park, and there are a number of small bridges connecting the two sections. There is an animal centre (part of which has an entry charge) housing guinea pigs, rabbits and pheasants, to name a few of the creatures you might encounter there. / Times: 7am-dusk; BR: Hanwell or 207 bus or E1 or E3 buses; Café, Picnic area.

Burnham Beeches

www.cityoflondon.gov.uk

Farnham Common   (01753) 647358

Though not quite IN London, this famous beauty spot – one of the finest examples of ancient woodland in Britain – can fairly claim to be OF the capital city as it has been owned by the Corporation of London since 1880. The most famous feature of the 540-acre site is the beech pollards, some of which are almost 500 years old. There is a programme of regular free walks and talks, and usually an annual open day in late June (check the website or call for details). The latter offers a chance to see displays of falconry, countryside management techniques and examples of country crafts. Given the wood's accessibility (just north of Junction 6 of the M4), it would be the perfect place to get away from it all, were it not for the fact that every year half a million other people have the same idea! Autumn is the very best time to visit. / Times: 8am-dusk; BR: Slough (then bus to Farnham Common).

Bushy Park

www.royalparks.gov.uk

White Lodge, The Stockyard, Bushy Park, Hampton Court Rd, Hampton Hill   (020) 8979 1586

This ancient deer park was laid out as part of Wren's grand design for neighbouring Hampton Court. Herds of red and fallow deer roam its 1,100 acres. The Woodland Gardens, with their fine azaleas, camellias and rhododendrons, are a post-war addition and make a nice place for a picnic. They boast a fine chestnut avenue which is the focal point of Chestnut Sun (May) – a traditional Victorian parade and picnic, celebrating the blossoming of the trees. / Times: pedestrians 24hrs (except Sep-Nov 8am-10.30pm), vehicles 6.30am-dusk; BR: Hampton Wick; Café.

Chelsea Harbour SW10

www.chelsea-harbour.co.uk
(020) 7225 9166   3–4B
This contemporary riverside marina development never seems to have lived up to its aspirations, but makes a pleasant place for a riverside walk. (Despite its relatively central location, the Harbour has a surprisingly far-away feel and – on a good day and with a little bit of imagination – is about as close as London gets to the French Riviera.) Reflecting the proximity of many of London's grander residential areas, the development has become a centre for interior design firms. They are largely 'trade only', but there is an annual open day in March, highlighting new trends in interior design. / Times: Design Centre Mon-Fri 9.30am-5pm; Tube: Earl's Court (then C3 bus).

Chiswick House* W4

www.chgt.org.uk
Burlington Ln   (020) 8995 5390   1–3A
The mainly wooded, 64-acre gardens of this fine neo-classical villa have suitably Italianate highlights – statues, temples, urns and obelisks – and there is also a lake and a cascade waterfall. The house (to which there is an entry charge) is run by English Heritage. NB As this guide goes to press, the property is in the throes of "one of the country's biggest and most ambitious garden restoration projects", intended, over a two-year period, "to restore the gardens to their full 18th century glory". Some areas of the garden may therefore be closed to visitors.
/ Times: garden 7am-dusk daily; information centre 9am-30 minutes before the park closes; Tube: Turnham Green (then E3 bus); Café, Picnic area.

Crane Park Island

www.wildlondon.org.uk
Crane Park, Twickenham   (020) 7261 0447
This small island (just over four acres), accessed by bridge, has its place in history – the old gunpowder mill here (now demolished) is believed to have been where Guy Fawkes obtained his supplies. Nowadays, its attractions are more peaceful, and it's an agreeable site, run by the London Wildlife Trust. Due to the cleanliness of its water, it is home to the rare water vole, and also safe for kids to paddle in. There are three paths, one of which (the Hobbin Path) is suitable for disabled people. During the summer holidays, there is a playscheme – call for details. / Times: 24 hours; BR: Whitton.

Garrick's Temple & Lawn at Hampton TW12

www.garrickstemple.org.uk

Hampton Court Rd, Hampton   (020) 8831 6000

This garden building on the Thames, a 10 minute walk from Hampton Court Palace, was built in 1755-6 by David Garrick — England's second most famous actor, dramatist and theatre manager — to commemorate his idol, William Shakespeare. After a recent restoration, the opportunity was taken to install a display traversing Garrick's acting career and his Hampton private life. / Times: Temple (Apr-Sep) Sun 2pm-5pm and by appt; lawn 7.30am-dusk daily ; BR: Hampton Court and then R68 bus or Hampton and then 111 or 216 bus.

Gunnersbury Triangle Nature Reserve W4

www.chiswickw4.com

Bollo Ln   (020) 8747 3881   1–3A

This six-acre site developed a rich covering of vegetation after being surrounded by railway tracks in the late c19. Since then it has been undisturbed, apart from some allotments, until it was threatened by development in the early '80s and became a 'test case'. The conservationists won, and this was the first time that a planning inspector had preferred nature conservation to development on a city site. It is now managed by the local volunteers of the London Wildlife Trust and during summer school holidays there is usually a full-time warden (daily) and a programme of free events. There is also a small information centre. / Tube: Chiswick Park.

Hampton Court Palace Gardens*

www.hrp.org.uk

(0870) 752 7777

The wonderful gardens and park of Wolsey's great riverside palace (completed by Henry VIII and substantially altered by William and Mary) are open to the public without charge. They include features from Victorian times, as well as from the earlier periods of the palace's construction, and a riverside walk. Around the gardens, in the 560-acre area that includes both Bushey and Home parks, graze the descendants of the deer hunted by Tudor monarchs. There is a charge for access to the Palace itself, the maze and the Privy Garden of William III. / Times: 10am-4.30pm daily ; BR: Hampton Court; Café.

Holland Park W8

www.rbkc.gov.uk

Ilchester Place   (020) 7602 2226   1–3B

Until the 1950s, Holland Park was an extraordinary hangover from former days — a private 'country' estate, in the middle of London. It maintains a unique and charming character, and, in spite of its relatively small size (52 acres), some of it is heavily wooded (and managed so as to enhance wildlife). Apart from its superb formal gardens, it benefits from the Kyoto Garden, installed by Japanese benefactors in 1991. Visit just before sunset to witness the peacocks' bedtime, when the birds fly into the trees and screech to one another. Other attractions include

*a large adventure playground and the Ecology Centre, which
has a series of free talks. There are also educational events for
organised groups (details from the Ecology Service) including
pond dipping for children, and a conservation programme for
volunteers of all ages. The Park contains the Orangery and the
Ice House.* / Times: winter 8am-4.30pm; summer 8am-9.30pm;
Tube: Holland Park, Kensington High Street; Café.

Hyde Park W2

www.royalparks.gov.uk
(020) 7298 2000   3–1C
*The greatest of the central Royal Parks was originally acquired
by Henry VIII from the Abbey at Westminster as a private
hunting ground. In 1637, when Charles I opened it to the
public, it became notorious as a haunt of footpads and thieves.
(William III later had 300 oil lamps erected to deter them,
creating Britain's first artificially-lit highway.) The giant glass
structure of Crystal Palace covered almost eight hectares of the
park when it was erected for the Great Exhibition of 1851.*

*The park's 344 acres now offer a variety of attractions, ranging
from the formal gardens along its south side, Rotten Row (a
bridleway for more than 300 years, its name derived from the
French 'Route du Roi'), a river (the Serpentine), and areas of
woods and grass. There is a children's playground and a Pet
Cemetery (open only one day a year in Sept; look for posters
around the park advertising the date). In 2004, a Diana
Memorial fountain was opened which aims to reflect the late
Princess of Wales's life through its design. In summer, there are
weekend and bank holiday concerts at the bandstand
(afternoons and evenings). Speakers' Corner (see also) is
situated in the north east corner of the park. Kensington
Gardens (see also) adjoin the park, and many more attractions
can be found there.* / Times: 6am-dusk; Diana Memorial Fountain
10am-8pm (Sep 7pm, Mar and Oct 6pm, Nov-Feb 4pm); Diana Memorial
Playground 10am-7.45pm (Apr and Sep 6.45pm, Mar and early Oct 5.45pm,
Feb and late Oct 4.45pm, Nov-Jan 3.45pm); Tube: Knightsbridge, Hyde Park
Corner, Marble Arch, Lancaster Gate, Queensway; Café, Picnic area.

Kensington Gardens W2

www.royalparks.gov.uk
(020) 7298 2117   3–1B
*These were the private gardens of Kensington Palace (designed
by Wren) and were largely laid out under the direction of
Queen Caroline in 1728. The gardens were opened to the
public by Queen Victoria and are effectively an extension of
Hyde Park (see also). Attractions in the 275 acres include the
Round Pond for boating (model boats only, please) where the
Model Boat Club meets every Sun morning, the charming small
statue of Peter Pan and the very pretty area in the immediate
vicinity of the Palace itself. The gardens also house the*

Serpentine Gallery and the Albert Memorial (see also). In
2000, the Diana Memorial Playground replaced one of the
original playgrounds. It is based on a Peter Pan theme and is
open 10am-dusk. In summer, there are weekly concerts at the
bandstand, occasional country dancing displays and children's
entertainments. / Times: dawn-dusk; Tube: Bayswater, Lancaster Gate,
Queensway, High Street Kensington; Café.

Kensington Roof Gardens W8

www.roofgardens.com
Barkers Department Store, Kensington High St (entrance
99 Derry St)   (020) 7937 7994   3–1A
Opened in the 1930s, this extraordinary 6th-floor installation is
Europe's largest roof garden (1.5 acres), and is most certainly
worth a visit. It is now home to a nightclub owned by Sir
Richard Branson, but (subject to prior club commitments)
daytime visitors are welcome. There are in fact three themed
adjoining gardens – an English woodland garden with
flamingos, a Tudor garden and a Spanish garden with palm
trees. / Times: 11am-5pm daily, but call ahead; Tube: High Street Kensington.

Marble Hill House*

www.guidetorichmond.co.uk
Richmond Rd, Twickenham   (020) 8892 5115
Built in the 1720s as a retreat from court life for Henrietta
Howard, Countess of Suffolk (George II's mistress), this
Palladian villa – one of the most perfect surviving examples of
the type – inhabits a park of 60 acres which stretches down to
the river. There is an admission charge for the house, but
access to the grounds is free. / Times: dawn-dusk; Tube: Richmond;
Café.

North End Road Market SW6

North End Rd   (020) 8748 3020   3–4A
Its not the loveliest stretch of road in Fulham, but there's
something grittily atmospheric about this large, haphazard
street market selling fruit, veg and bric-a-brac – one of the
largest in West London. At weekends the crush is so great it
can be difficult to make headway along the pavement.
/ Times: Mon-Sat 8am-6pm; Tube, Bus: Fulham Broadway.

Osterley Park*

www.nationaltrust.org.uk
Isleworth   (020) 8232 5050
Set in 140 acres of landscaped park and farmland with
ornamental lakes, this is one of the last great houses with an
intact estate in Greater London. Originally a c16 mansion (built
for Sir Thomas Gresham, founder of the Royal Exchange), it
was transformed into neo-classical style by Robert Adam in the
c18. Though the house has been a National Trust property for
over half a century, the trust only took over the management in
1990 (and both the grounds and garden house have recently
been refurbished). There is a charge for admission to the house
although access to the Jersey galleries is free. These house

temporary exhibitions of contemporary and local art (Mar-Oct).
Entrance is through the house so you get a glimpse of the
interior free of charge! There are also children's craft activities
during school holidays as well as occasional events such as
Osterley Day in June which has free activities for families. Call
the number above to find out about forthcoming events.
/ Times: 8am-6pm daily; Tube: Osterley; Café.

Portobello Road Market W10
www.portobelloroad.co.uk
1–2B
On Sat, Portobello market is undoubtedly the place in West
London for combining people-watching and browsing. The
street market stretches for over a mile, and in fact comprises
several different markets. The most famous, the antiques
market, is at the south end, but there is also a food market,
bric-à-brac stalls and (under the Westway) a good gathering of
vendors of trendy clothing and accessories. / Tube: Notting Hill Gate,
Ladbroke Grove.

Ranelagh Gardens SW3
Royal Hospital Rd   3–3D
Apart from when they are cordoned off every year (in May) for
the famous Chelsea Flower Show, the well-kept gardens
adjacent to the Royal Hospital lead a rather low-profile life.
They are, however, unusually pretty and intimate. A visit here
combines well with one to the neighbouring Royal Hospital (see
also). / Times: 10am (Sun 2pm)-30 mins before dusk, closed 1pm-2pm;
Tube: Sloane Square.

Ruislip Woods
www.hillingdon.gov.uk
Ruislip   (01895) 250635
There are a number of noteworthy features of these 700 acres
of woodland, including the 250-acre Park Wood, the largest
unbroken stretch of woodland in London. Ruislip Woodland
Centre covers the history of the area, which became a National
Nature Reserve in 1997. The centre also gives details of the
various species inhabiting the area – there are bats (at dawn
and dusk), woodpeckers, warblers and woodcocks to name a
few. A short guide to Ruislip Woods can be downloaded from
the website. / Times: Woodland Centre Sun 10am-4pm; Tube: Ruislip (then
331 bus); Café.

Shepherd's Bush Market W12
www.visitshepherdsbush.co.uk
Runs between Uxbridge Rd and Goldhawk Rd
(020) 8748 3079   1–3B
*Stretched out at the foot of and in the arches of the
Hammersmith & City line between Goldhawk Road and
Shepherd's Bush stations, this long narrow market sells a wide
variety of goods, fabrics and foods – most of it pretty cheaply.
There are over 300 stalls and shops, and the heady mix of
different Asian and African foodstuffs in some sections can
create an exotic atmosphere even in this most urban of
locations. / Times: Mon-Sat 9am-6pm (early close Thu); Tube,
Bus: Shepherds Bush.*

Speakers' Corner W2
Hyde Park (NE corner)   2–2A
*For more than a century, this has been the London home of the
soapbox orator – Sun sees the expression of a kaleidoscope of
views, from the slightly off-beat to the decidedly cranky.
/ Times: Sun morning; Tube: Marble Arch.*

North London

Introduction

North London's unique strength is the way it contains pockets of real nature, which seem to be only a stone's throw from the metropolis itself. The most obvious example is **Hampstead Heath**, but there is also **Highgate Wood** – and both are accessible by foot from the **Parkland Walk**, see also – and each is within a few tube stops of anywhere in central London.

In addition, there are many fine parks in the area. North London has its own Royal Park, in the form of **Regent's Park**, and its extension to the North, **Primrose Hill**, which has exceptional views over the city. **Alexandra Palace Park** gives yet another impressive perspective on the city below. The grounds of **Golders Green Crematorium** are a surprisingly fine amenity, relatively unknown to those outside the locality.

Few would dispute that Hampstead is by far the finest village in London, and two of its lovely period houses may be visited – **Burgh House** (whose museum gives the history of the area) and Keats House. The village's grandest residence, **Kenwood House**, at the top of the Heath, has an excellent period art collection.

For people who like being among people, the undoubted attraction is colourful **Camden Market**, which, every weekend, sprawls over the area from the Lock to the tube station. For children, it's probably the green spaces and the nature which are the main plus points. For the more inquisitive, however, the **Wellcome Collection** exhibitions offer an interesting diversion.

Harrow Tourist Information Centre
www.harrow.gov.uk
The Civic Centre, Station Rd, Harrow   (020) 8424 1102
The centre provides detailed information concerning local history, specific places of interest and nature preserves in Harrow. Local maps also are available. / Times: Mon-Fri 9am-5pm;
BR: Harrow & Wealdstone.

Suggested walk

For a taste of the varied nature of North London, set out for a stroll beginning in Regent's Park at the point where it meets the northern end of Baker Street. Head north – there are maps to guide you – and you will cross the entire width of the park, passing the boating lake to your left, Queen Mary's Gardens and the Zoo. Exiting the main northern entrance of the park, cross Regent's Canal and join Regent's Park Road. This winds along Primrose Hill, offering majestic views of London, as well as of stately houses and tree-lined streets. Continue walking until you reach Chalk Farm Road, with its array of eclectic shops and restaurants. Follow the road south – the activity increases as you reach Camden Lock and, at weekends, the bustling market. If the crowds prove too daunting, sneak down from the bridge at Camden Lock to Regent's Canal and walk east a mile or so to Camley Street Nature Park.

Indoor attractions

Barnet Museum
www.barnetmuseum.co.uk
31 Wood St, Barnet   (020) 8440 8066
A wide-ranging local history museum whose three or four annual temporary exhibits include shields from the Battle of Barnet – the penultimate battle in the Wars of the Roses.
/ Times: Tue-Thu 2.30pm-4.30pm, Sat 10.30am-12.30pm and 2pm-4pm;
Tube: High Barnet (then a half mile walk or 184 bus).

Brent Museum NW10
www.brent.gov.uk/museum
Willesden Green Library Centre, 95 High Rd
(020) 8937 3600   1–2A
The Brent Museum recently reopened in a new location, replacing its predecessor the Grange Museum. The new museum has a large number of objects and interactive displays giving Brent's history, and there are also temporary exhibitions. Their permanent exhibitions include items relating to transport, faith, the local area, a 1950s kitchen, and more. They are very interactive and family-friendly. On Wed during school holidays there are family events. / Times: Mon 11am-8pm, Tue and Thu 9am-8pm, Wed and Fri 9am-6pm, Sat 9am-6pm, Sun 11am-6pm;
Tube: Willesden Green.

British Library NW1

www.bl.uk

96 Euston Rd   (020) 7412 7000   4–3C

Does it look like an academy for secret policemen? That was the Prince of Wales's opinion on this striking building, home to every book published in the UK. You too can form a view of the architecture from the courtyard, but most of the library itself is reserved for those with reader cards. There is, however, a permanent exhibition gallery, exhibiting over 200 items, including such 'blockbusters' as Magna Carta, the Lindisfarne Gospels and a Gutenberg Bible. A second gallery hosts temporary exhibitions – see website for details. / Times: Mon, Wed, Thu, Fri 9.30am-6pm, Tue 9.30am-8pm, Sat 9.30am-5pm and Sun and bank hols 11am-5pm; Tube: King's Cross.

Bruce Castle Museum N17

www.haringey.gov.uk

Lordship Ln   (020) 8808 8772

Haringey's museum, with its wide collection of items of local interest, occupies an elegant and striking Grade I listed Tudor manor house. It was also once a school run by a Mr Hill and his sons (one of whom was called Roland), which operated on progressive lines (for its day) – for example, there was no corporal punishment and the children were involved in its administration. Roland grew up to be the inventor of the uniformed penny post – a postal history collection reflects his connection with the house.

Bruce Castle is located in two acres of parkland, containing a children's playground, bowling green, tennis court and basketball area. An interactive centre has recently been added. Sun 2pm-4pm, there are family activities, and the last Wed evening of each month, there are free talks and events (at 7pm). Temporary art exhibitions are held from time to time, and during the summer, there are regular arts and crafts activities. / Times: Wed-Sun 1pm-5pm; Tube: Wood Green (then 243 bus).

Burgh House & Hampstead Museum NW3

www.burghhouse.org.uk

New End Sq   (020) 7431 0144   4–1A

This handsome Queen Anne house (1703) is well worth a visit for its architecture, its pictures and its creaking charm. The ground floor is used as a community centre for the arts and houses temporary art exhibitions. The museum is on the first floor and has displays and objects about the history of Hampstead (long regarded as one of the most desirable places to live in or near the capital) and changing exhibitions on the history of the area. The house makes an ideal stopping-off point between the tube station and the Heath, and in the summer there is a nice garden to admire. / Times: Wed-Sun (and bank hols) noon-5pm (by appt on Sat); Tube: Hampstead; Café.

Camden Arts Centre NW3

www.camdenartscentre.org
Arkwright Rd   (020) 7472 5500   4–2A
The centre's three galleries hold about half a dozen contemporary art exhibitions a year. Top time to visit is Wed evening, when attractions may include artists' talks, film screenings and round table discussions. / Times: Tue-Sun 10am-6pm, Wed 10am-9pm; Tube: Finchley Road; Café.

Church Farmhouse Museum NW4

www.churchfarmhousemuseum.co.uk
Greyhound Hill   (020) 8359 3942
Built in 1660, this charming listed building (Hendon's oldest dwelling) combines permanent displays of c19 life with temporary exhibitions on local and social history and the decorative arts (and in December to February each year there's an exhibition especially for children). It has three reconstructed period rooms: kitchen (c1820); laundry room (c1890) and dining room (c1850). Every December, the dining room is decorated as if for a Victorian Christmas. / Times: Mon-Thu 10am-1pm and 2pm-5pm, Sat 10am -1pm and 2pm-5.30 pm, Sun 2pm-5.30pm; Tube: Hendon Central; Café, Restaurant, Picnic area.

Harrow Museum & Heritage Centre

www.harrow.gov.uk
Headstone Manor, Pinner View, Harrow   (020) 8861 2626
Originally built for the c14 Archbishops of Canterbury, this moated manor house has '30s interiors which are still in the course of renovation. It benefits from a pretty setting in a park, and there is also a c18 granary and a large and interesting c16 tithe barn. Here, a Victorian room setting, changing exhibitions and local history displays are on view, and there are lunchtime concerts on Sun. They also hold a "Fun House" every Wed afternoon from 2pm-2.45pm for children up to five years old to enjoy nursery rhymes and other activities. / Times: Mon, Wed, Thu, Fri noon-5pm, Sat, Sun 10.30am-5pm; Tube: Harrow-on-the-Hill (then H10 or H14 bus); Café, Picnic area.

Kenwood House NW3

www.english-heritage.org.uk
Hampstead Ln   (020) 8348 1286   4–1A
Perched like a grand wedding cake above Hampstead Heath, this neo-classical house (with Robert Adam façade, 1760s) provides a great cultural climax to a visit to the heath. The house (which was bequeathed to the nation by the first Earl of Iveagh in 1926) is certainly worth a view (the library is reckoned to be one of Adam's finest rooms), as are the artistic treasures within, which include a Rembrandt self-portrait and Vermeer's Guitar Player, as well as many famous works by Turner, Reynolds, Gainsborough, Van Dyck and Frans Hals. If you wander the paths on the estate, you might chance upon sculptures by Henry Moore and Barbara Hepworth. In the summer, open air concerts are held in the bowl by the lake – you can hear them from outside the pay-to-enter enclosure. / Times: 11.30am-4pm daily; Tube: Archway or Golders Green (then 210 bus); Café.

King's Place* N1

www.kingsplace.co.uk
90 York Way   (020) 7841 4860   4–3C
King's Place has been conceived an arts venue and creative hub
and its opening symbolises the arrival of a whole new city
quarter around King's Cross. It contains the first new public
concert hall to be built in central London since 1982. This hall
holds regular events, with occasional free concerts (see website
for dates). Kings Place has two galleries, the Pangolin London
and Kings Place Gallery. Pangolin London holds modern and
contemporary sculpture exhibitions and Kings Place Gallery has
a programme of temporary exhibitions. / Times: Mon-Sat
10am-7.30pm, Sun 11am-6.30pm; Tube: King's Cross; Café, Restaurant.

Lauderdale House Community Arts Centre* N6

www.lauderdalehouse.co.uk
Waterlow Park, Highgate Hill   (020) 8348 8716   1–1C
The three galleries of this Elizabethan house, set in the centre
of the attractive Waterlow Park, hold frequently changing
exhibitions. The centre holds regular performances (jazz,
cabaret, classical concerts and children's shows), workshops,
fairs and family events. Entry to the house and galleries is free
except when special exhibitions are held. Most shows and
workshops are free, although occasionally a fee is charged, so
it's generally best to call before you travel. / Times: Tue-Fri
11am-4pm, Sat 1.30pm-5pm, Sun noon-5pm (weekends subject to private
booking); Tube: Archway (then 143, 210 or 271 bus); Café.

London International Gallery of Children's Art
N19

www.ligca.org
Waterlow Park Centre, Dartmouth Park Hill
(020) 7281 1111   4–1C
In 2008, the London International Gallery of Children's Art
(LIGCA) moved to this new location in Waterlow Park Centre.
The LIGCA holds exhibitions of children's art from local
communities and from all over the world, and offers various
workshops and courses for ages two through twelve.
/ Times: Fri-Sun 10am-4pm, Mon-Sun workshops and birthday parties by appt;
Tube: Finchley Road.

Museum of Domestic Architecture & Design
1850–1950 N11

www.moda.mdx.ac.uk
Cat Hill, Barnet, Herts   (020) 8362 5244
The core of the six collections here is the Silver Studio, which
was one of the leading independent design studios from the
1880s until the 1960s. This collection includes wallpaper and
textile designs. Also of note: the library of Sir J M Richards (one
of the most important figures in c20 British architectural
history and a leading member of the Modern Movement in
Britain); the Peggy Angus Archive; the Sir Charles Hasler
Collection; the Crown Wallpaper Archive and the British and
Domestic Design Collection 1850-1950. / Times: Tue-Sat 10am (Sun
2pm)-5pm; Tube: Oakwood and then shuttlebus (runs every 20 mins) to
museum, Cockfosters; Café.

National Sound Archive NW1

www.bl.uk/nsa

British Library, 96 Euston Rd   (020) 7412 7440   4–3C

This is one of the largest sound archives in the world. The reception area has a touch-screen introduction to the facilities, and you can listen to examples of the material held. You can also pick up free leaflets and a newsletter. There is a library and information service, which includes catalogues of the holdings (both here and, for example, at the BBC) and historical information on recordings. For more fragile archives you need to pre-book to use their listening service equipment. The catalogue is available on the website. / Times: Mon 10am-8pm, Tue-Thu 9.30am-8pm, Fri and Sat 9.30am-5pm; Tube: King's Cross, Euston; Café, Restaurant.

Old Speech Room Gallery, Harrow School

www.harrowschool.org.uk

The Old Schools Building, Church Hill, Harrow-on-the-Hill (020) 8872 8205, (020) 8872 8000

The Old Speech Room of this famous school was built in 1819-21 as a place in which to encourage public speaking. In 1976, it was converted into a gallery to exhibit treasures accumulated over the years. There is a nucleus of antiquities, plus a series of temporary themed exhibitions which draw on highlights of the collection, such as c19 English watercolours, Modern British painting and some sculpture. For further information, including the dates of school holidays, visitors are advised to telephone. / Times: 2.30pm-5pm (closed Wed); closed school hols; Tube: Harrow-on-the-Hill (then 258 bus).

Royal Academy of Music Museum NW1

www.ram.ac.uk

Marylebone Rd   (020) 7873 7300   2–1A

The museum showcases the academy's collection of every variety of fine instrument, manuscripts and memorabilia. The star attraction is the selection of stringed instruments by the greatest Italian makers (most famously from the workshop of Stradivarius), and a whole floor dedicated to English pianos. You can watch instruments being worked on in the academy's maintenance shop and hear regular demonstrations of instruments in the collection. / Times: Mon-Fri 11.30pm-5.30pm, Sat-Sun noon-4pm; Tube: Baker Street; Café.

Royal Air Force Museum N9

www.rafmuseum.org.uk

Grahame Park Way   (020) 8205 2266   1–1A

A collection of aircraft, medals, uniforms, films and memorabilia pertaining to the RAF and to aviation in general. The Aeronauts Interactive Centre offers hands-on activities for all ages such as cockpit controls, air speed, drop zone, and pilot testing. The Battle of Britain Aircraft collection tells the story of the Royal Air Force's fight for control over the Channel with original aircraft and interactive displays. / Times: daily 10am-6pm (hours for exhibits may vary – see website for details); Tube: Colindale; Café, Restaurant, Picnic area.

Royal College of Physicians NW1

www.rcplondon.ac.uk

11 St Andrew's Place (020) 7935 1174 4–4B

You don't find many modern buildings that have already achieved the highest level (Grade I) listing, so this mid-'60s building (Sir Denys Lasdun), by Regent's Park, is of particular note. It's not only the architecture that makes it an interesting place to visit, though. There's a 'Heritage Centre', which includes a museum and an archive. / Times: Mon-Fri 9am-5pm, closed on bank hols and in Aug; archives and library by appt only; Tube: Regent's Park, Great Portland Street; Café, Restaurant, Picnic area.

Shri Swaminarayan Mandir NW10

www.swaminarayan.org

105-119 Brentfield Rd (020) 8965 2651 1–1A

The largest outside India (according to the Guinness Book of World Records), this intriguing Hindu temple is a peculiar addition to the skyline of the north-west London suburbs. It was inspired by the c18 guru, Lord Swaminarayan, who walked the length of India preaching the values of social care. The temple was built with the use of 2000 tons of Italian marble and nearly 3000 tons of Bulgarian limestone, which was all shipped to India to be shaped by more than 1000 skilled craftsmen before being brought to Neasden for assembly, thus being constructed by traditional means. For a small fee, visitors can see an exhibition about Hinduism and watch a 12-minute video explaining how and why the Mandir (place of worship) was constructed. / Times: 9am-6pm daily; Tube: Neasden; Café.

Stables Art Centre & Gallery NW2

www.gpcc.ik.com/p_Stablesprogramme1.ikml

Dollis Hill Ln (Gladstone Park) (020) 8452 8655 1–1A

A contemporary art gallery, housed in the former stables of Dollis Hill House, exhibiting works by local and national artists. / Times: Thu-Sun 11am-5pm; Tube: Dollis Hill or Neasden.

Stephens Collection N3

www.avenuehouse.org.uk

Avenue House, 15-17 East End Rd (020) 8346 7812

In 1918, Henry Charles 'Inky' Stephens bequeathed Avenue House and its grounds to the public. (Stephens Senior was the inventor of the famous blue-black writing fluid that writes blue and dries black, and which because of its indelible nature is still used for signing marriage registers.) Since 1993, Avenue House has housed a collection of artefacts relating to ink and ink products, including original enamel signs, quill and steel-nibbed pens. / Times: Tue-Thu 2pm-4.30pm and by appt; Tube: Finchley Central; Picnic area.

Wellcome Collection NW1

www.wellcomecollection.org

183 Euston Rd (020) 7611 2222 4–4C

The trust – headquarters of one of the richest charities in the world – houses three new galleries hosting two permanent exhibitions. These are "Medicine Man", which has items such as Napoleon's toothbrush and George III's hair, and "Medicine Now", which touches upon such topics as malaria and obesity. In addition to these permanent exhibits, there is usually at least one temporary exhibition. Various guided tours of the collection are offered. / Times: Tue-Wed, Fri-Sun 10am-6pm, Thu 10am-10pm; Tube: Euston, Euston Square; Café.

White Cube N1
www.whitecube.com
48 Hoxton Square   (020) 7930 5373   5–1D
Established in 2000, this striking commercial gallery was the arrival which put beyond doubt the fact that Hoxton had become home to the new art establishment. Its lofty space often exhibits the work of famous contemporary artists. / Times: Tue-Sat 10am-6pm; Tube: Old Street.

Outdoor attractions

Abney Park Cemetery N16
www.abney-park.org.uk
Stoke Newington High St   (020) 7275 7557   1–1C
A surprisingly countrified place (originally laid out as an arboretum), this cemetery that doubles as a nature reserve took over (around 1840) from Bunhill Fields as the final resting place of London's dissenters and non-conformists. General Booth, founder of the Salvation Army, is among those interred here, along with James Braidwood, first Superintendent of the London Fire Engine Establishment. The main entrance has been restored and there is a visitor centre which has information boards covering the geology of the stones of the site, its history and the (mainly local) characters buried here. Throughout the year there are various nature-related events, which you can check out on the website. / Times: summer 8am-7pm, winter 8am-4pm; visitor centre generally 10am-7pm; BR: Stoke Newington.

Alexandra Palace Park N22
www.alexandrapalace.com
Alexandra Palace Way   (020) 8365 2121
This 196 acre park is set around the vast Victorian Alexandra Palace. The park has woodlands, formal gardens, playing fields, meadows and conservation areas. Animals inhabiting the park include birds, bats, and foxes. It is easy to keep busy at the park with a children's play area and skate park, boating lake and fishing area and two cafés. There are frequently events at the park, some free, such as the Spring Bank Holiday Funfair. / Times: 24 hours; Tube: Wood Green (then W3 bus or free shuttle service available most days).

Batchworth Lock Canal Centre
www.rwt.org.uk
99 Church St, Rickmansworth   (01923) 778382
Batchworth Lock is an historic site on the Grand Union Canal. Located in former stables, the centre provides guides, leaflets and maps showing the network of waterways around Batchworth. One can also visit the narrow boat 'Roger'. (Looking round is free, but there is a small charge for excursions.) / Times: Tue-Fri 10am-4pm, Sat and Sun noon-5pm; Tube: Rickmansworth; Café.

Camden Lock NW1
www.camdenlockmarket.com
Chalk Farm Rd   (020) 7284 2084   4–2B
The slightly more upmarket side of Camden Market, with fashions, jewellery, books and crafts among the enormous variety of items on display. The lock is open all week, but, as with the rest of the market, Sat and Sun are the peak times for a visit. There are frequent summer attractions (generally during the week), such as street theatre, music and art shows – check website for details. / Times: 10am-6pm daily; Tube: Camden Town, Chalk Farm; Café, Restaurant.

Camden Market NW1
www.camdenlock.net
Camden High St (and surrounding area)   (020) 7485 8355   4–2B
At the weekend, the whole of hip young London seems to descend on Camden for its vibrant markets – together with the tourists, they make it one of the most visited attractions in town. (In fact, the Underground stations are closed for much of the day due to overcrowding, so be prepared to walk, or know the bus routes!) By no means are prices particularly bargain basement though, and unless you are shopping for the latest style, the real point of the trip is to stroll around window-shopping, people-watching and listening to the omnipresent musical beats. As with all crowded markets, keep a close eye on your belongings. / Times: Mon-Sun 9.30am-6pm ; Tube: Camden Town, Chalk Farm.

Camley Street Natural Park NW1
www.wildlondon.org.uk
12 Camley St   (020) 7833 2311   4–3C
In the heart of ever-changing King's Cross – on Regent's Canal (though not accessible from it) – this community nature reserve, run by the London Wildlife Trust, is also a designated Local Nature Reserve. Habitats include a marsh, a pond and a wood. There are some free events here during the year, for example the Spring Fun Days, Frog Day and the Camley Street Apple Day in October. There is an ongoing educational programme and a variety of children's events take place year-round – check the website, or call for details. Donations are appreciated. / Times: Mon-Sun 10am-5pm; Tube: King's Cross; Picnic area.

Chapel Market N1

Liverpool Rd (020) 7289 4371 4–3D

This diverse street market on the fringes of Islington is most popular at weekends and sells fruit, vegetables, fish, flowers and plants as well as a limited variety of general goods including fabrics and clothing. / Times: Tue-Wed, Fri-Sat 9am-3.30pm, Thu and Sun 9am-3pm; Tube: Angel.

Coldfall Wood N10

www.haringey.gov.uk

Creighton Av (020) 8348 6005

These 35 acres of ancient woodland to the north of Muswell Hill are of great ecological interest, and demonstrate examples of the returning fashion for traditional coppice management. If you intend to explore, call the Conservation Office who can provide you with further information, and the leaflet, Historic Woodlands in Haringey. / Tube: East Finchley.

Finsbury Park N4

www.haringey.gov.uk

Seven Sisters Rd (020) 8802 2612 4–1D

A large part of the 115 acres of this Victorian park is taken up with various sports facilities and a boating lake, so there's often a lot of activity. (You can even go fishing – but there's a charge for a licence.) New facilities include a dog-free play area, water feature, a new café building, and two Victorian-style seating shelters. There are several playgrounds, and a variety of small-scale children's events throughout the year, such as Easter egg hunts and fireworks night. (For more information, ring the Finsbury Park Action Group on the number given.) / Times: 6.30am-dusk; Tube: Finsbury Park; Café.

Freightliners Farm N7

www.freightlinersfarm.org.uk

Sheringham Rd (020) 7609 0467 4–2D

This three-and-a-half acre city farm in Islington is among the oldest in London. Amongst the usual farm animals are some rare breeds, and attractions also include an ornamental garden. There are many different activities: from sessions for under-4's to carpentry, horticulture, permaculture, animal husbandry, and straw-bale building. There's an 'Open Day' on the second bank holiday in May, where the attractions include sheepdog trials, sheep-shearing demonstrations, country crafts and children's activities. / Times: Tue-Sun 10am-4pm (spring and summer 4.45pm); Tube: Highbury & Islington, Holloway Road; Café, Restaurant, Picnic area.

Fryent Country Park NW9

www.london.gov.uk

Fryent Way, Kingsbury 1–1A

For those in search of real country in town, these 260 acres of unspoilt rural farmland, sandwiched between Wembley and Kingsbury, are pretty much the perfect answer. Nature walks, ponds and a wildlife area are among the attractions. / Times: 24 hours; Tube: Kingsbury, Wembley Park.

North London

Gladstone Park NW10
www.brent-heritage.co.uk
Dollis Hill Ln 1–1A
William Gladstone was a frequent visitor to the fine Dollis Hill House (1824) which forms the centrepiece of this very varied 100-acre park between Neasden and Willesden. Other attractions include an arboretum filled with hundreds of exotic trees from all over the world, a pond with ducks and geese, and an old walled garden. / Times: 8am–dusk; Tube: Neasden, Dollis Hill.

Golders Green Crematorium NW11
Hoop Ln   (020) 8455 2374   1–1B
For the casual observer, spring is the time to visit this fine crematorium, set in 12 acres of landscaped grounds. At that time of the year, the front lawns are covered with upwards of 100,000 crocus. Founded in 1902, the building features unusual northern Italianate architecture (by Sir Ernest George, RA, who also designed Claridge's Hotel). Those who have been cremated here include Marc Bolan, Gustave Holst, Charles Rennie Mackintosh, Sigmund Freud, Ronnie Scott, Peter Cook and Anna Pavlova. / Times: 9am–6pm (winter 4pm); Tube: Golders Green; Café.

Golders Hill Park NW11
www.camden.gov.uk
West Heath Rd   (020) 7332 3511   1–1B
A pretty, landscaped park whose main attraction is a small zoo, with deer, wallabies, goats and sheep. There is also a duck pond, woods and tennis courts. / Times: 7.30am–30 mins before dusk; Tube: Golders Green; Café, Picnic area.

Hampstead & Highgate Ponds NW3
Hampstead Heath   (020) 7485 5757   4–1A
Hampstead Heath boasts over 20 ponds – and you can swim in three of them. During the season (from the first Sat before the May bank holiday to the third Sun in September) you can choose between the Hampstead Pond (mixed), the Highgate Pond (men) and the Kenwood Pond (women). Showers and changing areas are available. All ponds limit children to those aged eight and over, and to one per adult. Swimmers who do not appear to be 'competent' may be asked to leave. See also Parliament Hill Lido. / Times: summer, mixed 7am–7pm, single sex 7pm–9pm (or sunset if earlier); winter, call to check; Tube: Hampstead, Kentish Town (then 214 or C2 bus).

Hampstead Heath NW3
www.cityoflondon.gov.uk
(020) 7332 3322   4–1A
Hampstead Heath's 791 acres, administered by the Corporation of London, offer everything from a fine c18 house complete with art collection with formal gardens – Kenwood (see also) – to heathland which is as close as you get to real countryside near central London. There are also tremendous vistas – the views of the metropolis from some parts of the heath are so fine they have special legal protection. Other attractions include the bathing pools (see Hampstead &

*Highgate Ponds), concerts at the bandstand on Golders and
Parliament Hills, free talks and walks. For kids there is a
playpark, and a programme of free entertainment including
Punch and Judy, magicians and clowns. A full diary of events is
available with an A5 SAE every March from The Parliament
Hill Staff Yard, Highgate Road, London NW5 1PL. / Times: 24
hours; Tube: Hampstead, Golders Green.*

Highgate Wood N6
www.cityoflondon.gov.uk
Muswell Hill Rd   (020) 8444 6129
*The 70 acres of Highgate Wood were taken over by the
Corporation of London as "an open space for ever" in 1886.
There's a small playground and a sports ground, but the
attraction is essentially what the name suggests – an ancient
woodland, with diverse flora and fauna, all just a few yards
from the Archway Road. If you're planning to spend more than
an hour or so in the wood, collect or send for a copy of the
attractively illustrated free booklet, 'Highgate Wood', which lists
the flora, birds and butterflies which can be spotted there. This,
a newsletter and other leaflets on woodpecker trails, bat
conservation trusts and the local natural history are available
from the information hut or with an A5 SAE from Corporation
of London, Highgate Wood, Muswell Hill Road, London N10
3JN. You might also like to explore the neighbouring 48-acre
Queen's Wood (across the Muswell Hill Road), which is
relatively wild and boasts an equally impressive selection of
wildlife. (Both areas are part of the Parkland Walk, see also.)
The information centre organises free walks and talks on an
occasional basis – see website for details. / Times: 7.30am-dusk;
Tube: Highgate.*

Kentish Town City Farm NW5
www.aapi.co.uk/cityfarm
1 Cressfield Close, Grafton Rd   (020) 7916 5421   4–2B
*A working farm of some four acres, with many typical farm
animals and a wide range of activities for children. Opened in
1972, it was the first of its kind to be established and has
played an important role in the development of the City Farm
movement. / Times: Tue-Sun 9am-5.30pm; Tube: Chalk Farm, Kentish Town.*

Parkland Walk (Railway Fields Nature Park)
(020) 8348 6005
*Walking down a railway track might seem a rather hazardous
activity, but the redundant line between Finsbury Park station
and Alexandra Palace is actually a Local Nature Reserve and
offers an interesting alternative for a country walk in town. The
total length of the walk is four and a half miles and takes
around two hours. It is worth getting the free leaflet (which
includes a map, available from the Haringey Conservation
Officer on the number given) to avoid getting lost in Highgate
Wood, or giving up when confronted with the very unpark-like
Archway Road. / Tube: Finsbury Park (south section), Highgate (middle),
Alexandra Palace; BR or W3 bus back to Finsbury Park (north).*

Primrose Hill NW3

www.primrosehill.com

(020) 7486 7905   4–3B

The hill – the 206-ft high continuation of Regent's Park to the north – is by far the most central natural vantage point over London, and is therefore justly celebrated for its views (and is one of the six legally protected viewpoints in the capital). When there's enough snow, it's an extremely atmospheric place to go tobogganing. There has been an outdoor gymnasium on the site since Victorian times and there are still fifteen types of exercise equipment available for year-round use. To get you in the mood, the walk along the towpath of the Regent's Canal from Camden Lock or Little Venice is a nice way of approaching the hill. / Times: dawn-dusk; Tube: Chalk Farm, Camden Town.

Queen's Park NW6

www.cityoflondon.gov.uk

Kingswood Av   (020) 8969 5661   1–2B

A 30-acre Kilburn park owned and run by the Corporation of London since 1886. It's not particularly large, but popular in this relatively under-provided part of town, and especially good for children, thanks to its large, supervised playground and its paddling pool. There is also an ornamental garden and a fine Victorian bandstand. The second Sun in September sees the annual Queen's Park Day – involving music, comedy, games and a carnival – which draws big crowds. During school holidays, the park offers children's shows and storytelling events. / Times: 7am-dusk; Tube: Queen's Park.

Railway Fields Local Nature Reserve N4

www.haringey.gov.uk

Opposite Haringey/Green Lanes Station

(020) 8348 6005   1–1C

This conservation park, in a former British Rail goods coal yard, has been developed for teaching primary school children about nature. There is a meadow, a woodland and a pond, and even a unique hybrid plant- the Haringey Knotwead. A visitor centre, with leaflets, provides information about the ecology of the site (as well as other places of environmental interest in the borough). / Times: Mon-Fri 10am-5pm (phone to confirm); Tube: Manor House.

Regent's Canal Towpath

www.britishwaterways.co.uk

(020) 7985 7780

Created as part of Nash's design for Regent's Park, these eight or so miles of the canal run from Paddington, along the north of the park, through Camden at Camden Lock, and on to the waterway's conclusion in Docklands in the east, where it joins the Thames at the Limehouse Basin. There is a towpath along its entire length which passes through tunnels and alongside locks, and past the perimeter of parts of London Zoo. The prettiest part is towards its western conclusion in the stretch through Little Venice W9. You can download a guide from www.waterscape.com. / *Tube: Camden Town (eastern end), Paddington (west), Warwick Avenue (Little Venice).*

Regent's Park NW1
www.royalparks.gov.uk
(020) 7486 7905   4–3B

Regent's Park's 297 acres have an atmosphere all of their own, perhaps because the park was in fact designed as a grand garden suburb. In the end, only eight of the 26 villas which John Nash planned at the beginning of the c19 were built (though a few more have subsequently been added). Queen Mary's Gardens have one of the finest selections of blooms in the country, including the Eudia, a very rare tree, and the lake boasts an impressive variety of wildfowl. The annual Music Village (early July) is Britain's longest-running 'festival of living traditions from around the world' and is a platform for international popular music, dance and crafts. During the summer, music is performed on a regular basis at the bandstand or at various other points around the park at weekends and some evenings during the week. There are also children's workshops during school holidays. / *Times: 5am-dusk; Tube: Regent's Park, Baker Street, Camden Town, Great Portland Street; Café, Restaurant, Picnic area.*

Roundwood Park NW10
www.brent.gov.uk
Robson Av, Harlesden Rd   (020) 8838 1414   1–2A

A fine grade II listed 60-acre Victorian park in Willesden that has impressive floral displays and an aviary stocked with exotic birds. There is also a children's playground. / *Times: 8am-dusk; Tube: Willesden Green; Café.*

Waterlow Park N6
www.waterlowpark.org.uk
Islington   1–1C

Given to the public by Sir Sydney Waterlow in 1889, this 'garden for the gardenless' is situated on a steep hillside and has an unusual three-level lake, formal gardens and terraces. Lauderdale House (see also) is within the park. Facilities include a children's play area. / *Times: 7.30am-dusk; Tube: Highgate*

South London

Introduction

South London boasts many of the best free destinations, especially for a family day out. Indeed, in **Tate Modern** the area boasts what is now the capital's second most popular attraction.

Just over Chelsea Bridge, **Battersea Park** is the only one of the central parks to benefit from a river frontage, and offers a wide range of attractions. A little further south, **Dulwich Park** is very fine. **Crystal Palace Park** is also an interesting destination (especially on a Sunday or a bank holiday afternoon, when the Museum is open).

To the south east – Greenwich – with **Greenwich Park**, the **Old Royal Naval College** and the **Old Royal Observatory** – makes an excellent destination for a day out (with the **Thames Barrier** not far away). To the south west, Richmond, and the great adjoining **Richmond Park** is also a very attractive place for a full day's exploration (especially bearing in mind the attractions around Twickenham, just on the other side of the river – see West).

If you're heading back to central London from some of the cultural attractions south of the river, such as the **Imperial War Museum**, it's worth bearing in mind that the early evening sees some of London's best free music, at the **Royal National Theatre** and the **Royal Festival Hall** – posters on the South Bank list all the free events for the current month.

Greenwich Tourist Information Centre SE10
www.greenwich.gov.uk
Pepys House, 2 Cutty Sark Gardens   (020) 8858 6376
/ *Times: Mon-Sun 10am-5pm; DLR: Cutty Sark.*

Lewisham Tourist Information Centre SE13
www.lewisham.gov.uk
199-201 Lewisham High St   (020) 8297 8317
/ *Times: Mon 10am-5pm, Tue-Sat 9am-5pm; BR: Lewisham, Ladywell.*

Richmond Community & Information Centre
www.visitrichmond.co.uk
The Old Town Hall, Whittaker Av, Richmond
(020) 8940 9125
/ *Times: Mon-Sat 10am-5pm; Tube: Richmond.*

Riverside walks

Arguably the finest walking in London, and certainly some of its best vistas, can be enjoyed on the mostly continuous paths which run along the Thames, on both the north and south banks from Kingston in the west to Docklands in the east.

The south bank is, on balance, the better place to walk, because it is generally more peaceful and it gives views of the almost invariably more picturesque north bank. (If you get bored, the distances between bridges are generally quite short so you can always swap sides.)

The most rural-feeling of the more central stretches of the river is the (often muddy) towpath on the south bank between Putney Bridge and Barnes Bridge. A good route to try begins at the half-way point, at Hammersmith Bridge – walk down to Barnes Bridge and circle back on the north bank (which is also attractive in this area). There are many good pubs at Hammersmith, some with a river view, so you might like to time your return to coincide with lunch.

If it's a walk in the centre of town you're after, there is a fine continuous stretch between the Houses of Parliament and Tower Bridge, along Victoria Embankment (the north bank of the river). In the City the walk leads you past the picturesque Tower of London to St Katharine's Dock (see also).

For another stroll on the same stretch of river, one of the nicest places, not least because it is away from the traffic, is along the south bank from Westminster Bridge – there are magnificent views (especially of the Houses of Parliament and St Paul's) and it is a particularly nice walk at sunset. Some of the best views in London is from the new twin footbridges either side of Hungerford railway bridge (between Embankment Tube and the South Bank Centre).

Heading east from County Hall and the impressive Millennium Wheel, you will pass the South Bank Centre and National Theatre. The second-hand bookstall under Waterloo Bridge is a great place to stop and browse. Beyond this is Gabriel's Wharf – with attractive gardens and a shopping area, it is particularly busy on a sunny day – and the ITV television studios. Continue east, past the Oxo Tower, which brings you to the area now known as 'Bankside' – Tate Modern and the impressive reconstruction of Shakespeare's Globe Theatre are features. End at the famous 'wobbly' Millennium footbridge, and the walk across the river to St Paul's provides a truly dramatic finale.

South London

As you near London Bridge, the river path diverts inland, taking you along the atmospheric Clink Street, towards Southwark Cathedral and Borough Market – this area gets quite crowded at weekends. If you wander even further east, you will be able to see Tower Bridge in the distance, and will pass Lord Foster's City Hall building.

Other Thames-side walks to consider include a stroll along the riverside path in Battersea Park (see also), the north bank to the east of Kew Bridge, and, further out of town, the extremely pretty stretch at Richmond – there is quite a number of riverside pubs to distract you.

Indoor attractions

Addington Palace
www.addington-palace.co.uk
Gravel Hill, Croydon   (020) 8662 5000
The Palace – home in its day to six Archbishops of Canterbury – was built in 1776 for Barlow Tregothick, Lord Mayor of London. It is set in a 'Capability' Brown landscape and is of interest both for its architecture and its history. Parts of the Palace were restored in 1900 by Norman Shaw and the décor of the rooms dates from then. The Great Hall is lined with polished Italian walnut and the impressive fireplace is made from Italian marble. Now a conference and banqueting suite, the palace is open six days a year for free guided tours – call or check the website for details. / Times: free open days throughout year (see below) Sun or Mon 2pm-4.30pm ; BR: East Croydon (then 466 bus or no.3 tram); Café.

Age Exchange Reminiscence Centre SE3
www.age-exchange.org.uk
11 Blackheath Village   (020) 8318 9105   1–4D
The highlight here is the charming '30s general shop with its genuine fittings and original stock. This "hands-on museum of the 1930s and 1940s" should interest anyone who can remember those days, as well as those who cannot. There is a changing temporary exhibition at the rear. The café serves tea and cakes in period style – in the garden in fine weather. For large groups visiting, a donation is asked for. / Times: Mon-Sat 10am-5pm ; BR: Blackheath; Café.

Bargehouse SE1
www.coinstreet.org
Oxo Tower Wharf, Bargehouse St   (020) 7021 1600
5–3A
A wander around the design shops of Oxo Tower combines well with a visit to the Bargehouse (admission to the gallery is free but some exhibitions may charge). Contemporary international artists from all disciplines are represented, and the exhibitions change every three weeks (see also the riverside walk).
/ Times: 11am-6pm daily during exhibitions; Tube: Blackfriars, Southwark, Waterloo; Café, Restaurant.

Beaconsfield Contemporary Art SE11
www.beaconsfield.ltd.uk
22 Newport St   (020) 7582 6465   1–3C
*Most exhibitions are free at this contemporary gallery located
in the former Lambeth Ragged School, in Vauxhall. The gallery
sponsors solo installations by artists as well as group shows,
sometimes in collaboration with other international
organisations.* / Times: hours vary by exhibition, call to check (generally
11am-6pm); Tube: Vauxhall, Lambeth North, Waterloo; Café.

Bethlem Royal Hospital Archives & Museum
www.bethlemheritage.org.uk
Monks Orchard Rd, Beckenham   (020) 3228 4307
*Founded in 1247, Bethlem Royal Hospital, was home to many
paintings and drawings by artists who have suffered mental
disorder, some of whom were confined there. These include
works by artist Richard Dadd (1817-1886), who spent 42
years in criminal lunatic asylums, the dancer Nijinsky, and one
Jonathan Martin whose prophetic dreams led him to set fire to
York Minster in 1829. In addition, the museum has some
material relating to the history of Bethlem. It will move to a
new building, on the same site, in 2010.* / Times: Mon-Fri
9.30am-4.30pm; BR: Eden Park, or East Croydon (then 119, 194, or 198 bus);
Café.

Bexley Heritage Trust
www.bexleyheritagetrust.org.uk
Hall Place, Bourne Rd, Bexley   (01322) 526574
*Formerly known as Bexley Museum, the building is part Tudor
and part Jacobean and is set in extensive gardens and
nurseries on the bank of River Cray. The museum contains
displays of local geology, natural history and archaeology, plus a
mock-up of a Victorian bath! There are varied temporary
exhibitions, mostly on a local history theme, and modern arts
and crafts displays.* / Times: Mon-Sat 10am-5pm (winter 4.15pm), Sun
2pm-6pm (summer); BR: Bexley, Bexley Heath; Café.

Borough Market SE1
www.boroughmarket.org.uk
8 Southwark St   (020) 7407 1002   5–4C
*Since 1754 there's been a fruit and veg market at this South
Bank location, occupying a hugely atmospheric Victorian
structure set into the railway arches near London Bridge
station. (Rail planners perennially threaten to flatten it to
improve journey times.) Prior to 1998, it was primarily of
interest to the wholesalers, who ply their trade from 10pm to
8am nightly. The last few years, though, has since the
establishment of a hugely popular "Fine Food Fair" which
operates on Thu, Fri and Sat. Food producers from all over the
UK (and Europe) set up over 60 stalls, from which you can 'try*

and buy' goods from cheese to organic chocolate. The very characterful surrounding area (especially Park Street) has also been colonised by gourmet food shops, so foodies can now window shop all week long. Southwark Festival's annual food festival is also held here (see also). / Times: Thu 11am-5pm, Fri noon-6pm, Sat 9am-4pm; Tube: London Bridge, Borough; Café, Restaurant, Picnic area.

Bromley Museum
www.bromley.gov.uk/leisure/museums
The Priory, Church Hill, Orpington   (01689) 873826
This local history museum is housed in a largely medieval building, set in attractive gardens. Exhibitions, which take place in the Great Hall and change four to five times per year, include paintings and crafts by locals. The permanent exhibitions are housed upstairs and include "Bromley's Past", and the Avebury Room which commemorates Sir John Lubbock, the first Lord Avebury (1834-1913), whom we have to thank for bank holidays. There are also a number of free family events throughout the year which usually coincide with school holidays. / Times: Mon-Sat 10am-5pm, Sun and bank hols 1pm-5pm (1 Nov-31 Mar closed Sun and bank hols); BR: Orpington; Café.

Brooking Collection SE10
www.gre.ac.uk
University of Greenwich (Maritime Campus), Pepys Stable Block, Old Royal Naval College   (020) 8331 9312   1–3D
Windows rescued from Windsor, doorknobs from 10 Downing Street ..., this unique and comprehensive collection, amassed by Charles Brooking over 35 years, contains over 100,000 architectural details from the past five centuries including doors, staircase sections, bootscrapers and rainwater hoods. Many visitors to the collection come because they inhabit a period property which they want to restore or refurbish and want a point of reference. Information on more than 7,000 items is held on computer and examples of details of specific types or particular periods can be retrieved prior to the visit. / Times: by appt 9am-5pm (also weekends for groups); BR: Maze Hill.

City Hall SE1
www.london.gov.uk
The Queen's Walk   (020) 7983 4000   5–4D
The home of Mr Mayor and the GLA, this extraordinary building was designed by Norman Foster and opened in 2002. Part of it is open to the general public, including the exhibition space from where one can view the Assembly Chamber. In addition, all the meetings of the Mayor's Advisory Cabinet, the London Assembly and its committees including the Mayor's Question Time are open to the public. There is a public information desk in the Lower Ground floor (Mon-Fri 9.30am-5pm) which can provide details. If you would like a short talk outlining the role of the GLA, contact the Public Liaison Unit, (020) 7983 4100. The building is also generally open on the first weekend of every month – check the website. / Times: Mon-Fri 8am-8pm; Tube: Tower Hill; Café.

Crystal Palace Museum SE19
www.crystalpalacemuseum.org.uk
Anerley Hill   (020) 8676 0700
The museum tells the story of the Crystal Palace, erected as a temporary structure in Hyde Park as the centrepiece of the Great Exhibition of 1851. The glass building attracted much interest and was moved to Upper Norwood, where it stood until it burned down in 1936. The museum is housed in a brick-built part of the original structure. Exhibits are mainly photographs, including pictures of the fire, as well as some Victorian souvenirs. The museum is set in 200 acres of parkland – see also Crystal Palace Park. / Times: Sat and Sun 11am-4.30pm; BR: Crystal Palace.

Cuming Museum SE17
www.southwark.gov.uk
151 Walworth Rd   (020) 7525 2332   1–3C
Southwark is one of the most historically interesting parts of London. Its museum (just south of Elephant & Castle) has a rather unusual basis, being derived largely from the objects collected by the Cuming family between 1786 and 1902. The Cuming Museum moved to a new site in 2006. It holds new exhibits every 6-9 months. Two new permanent exhibitions explore the Cuming family collection and the story of Southwark. Both exhibitions have hands-on activities for children, including dressing up and handling replicas. / Times: Tue-Sat 10am-5pm; Tube: Elephant & Castle; Café, Restaurant, Picnic area.

De Morgan Centre SW18
www.demorgan.org.uk
38 West Hill LIbrary, West Hill   (020) 8871 1144   1–4B
An extensive collection of the works of William and Evelyn de Morgan, together with archival material relating to themselves and their circle. He was part of the Arts and Crafts movement and – though best-known for his ceramic tiles – also painted, designed stained glass, and later wrote novels. She was a painter, whose style was heavily influenced by fellow pre-Raphaelite, Edward Burne-Jones. / Times: Tue-Wed noon-6pm, Fri-Sat 10am-5pm; BR: Wandsworth.

Deen City Farm SW19
www.deencityfarm.co.uk
39 Windsor Ave, Merton Abbey   (020) 8543 5300
Animals at this five-acre city farm range from the expected to rare breeds, and there is also an expanding pure breed poultry programme. The emphasis is on seeing and touching, and there are also information boards. On weekends, there are barn owl and reptile demonstrations. An upcoming project is the incorporation of a Sensory Garden, which will provide a number of impacts on visitors' senses through sight, smell, touch and hearing. Donations are appreciated. / Times: Tue-Sun 10am-4.30pm; BR: Wimbledon (then 200 bus to Fips Bridge), Collingswood, South Wimbledon; Tramlink: Morden Road, Fips Bridge; Café.

George Inn SE1
www.nationaltrust.org.uk
77 Borough High St   (020) 7407 2056   5–4C
The only remaining galleried coaching inn in London is c17 in origin and was mentioned by Dickens in Little Dorritt. It is still a public house (leased by the National Trust to Whitbread) so anyone can go and have a look at its interior. Parts are extremely characterful and include the tavern clock which dates back to 1745. There are Morris dancing displays in the courtyard in the summer, and at around 8pm on the first Mon of the month (not bank hols) a group plays traditional English music. / Times: Mon-Sat 11am-11pm, Sun noon-10.30pm; Tube: London Bridge.

Greenwich Heritage Centre SE18
www.greenwichheritage.org
Artillery Square, Woolwich   (020) 8854 2452   1–3D
It's 'all change' at this local museum, which moved in the autumn of 2003 from the upper floor of Plumstead Library to new premises at Woolwich Arsenal. The Heritage Centre brings together the former Borough Museum and Local History Library to offer information on the history of Greenwich. They have a large collection of books, photographs, drawings, and maps. Their free exhibition 'Inside the Arsenal' tells the story of the Royal Arsenal and the surrounding area through the lives of the people who lived and worked there. The Centre also offers activities and events, many for a small fee, however their Children's Sat Club is free. / Times: Tue-Sat 9am-5pm; Tube: North Greenwich.

Hall Place & Hall Place Gardens, Kent
www.hallplace.org.uk
Bourne Rd, Bexley   (01322) 526574
Hall Place, a Grade I listed country house, was built in 1540 for Sir John Champneis (a Lord Mayor of London), and extended in the c17. Almost all the rooms are open to the public, including the beautiful Great Hall. The building also houses Bexley Heritage Trust (see also – formerly known as Bexley Museum) and galleries with regularly changing exhibitions. The award-winning formal gardens are laid out on either side of the River Cray and feature a Tudor-style rose garden, a herb garden and a topiary display depicting chess pieces and twelve heraldic animals known as the 'Queen's Beasts'. / Times: 10am-4pm daily; BR: Bexley Village.

Honeywood Museum*
www.friendsofhoneywood.co.uk
Honeywood Walk, Carshalton   (020) 8770 4297
Alas, this c17 house (with Victorian and Edwardian additions), on the edge of the Carshalton Village ponds, is no longer generally free to enter. However, there are at least three days a

year when access won't cost you anything. These include the anniversary of the museum (usually the first Sun in December) and the Heritage Open Weekend (mid-September, with free tours of the house and gardens). When you do get in you'll find an exhibition setting out the history of the borough (Sutton), including an audiovisual display. Many of the rooms have been refurbished in period style. / Times: §; BR: Carshalton; Café.

Horniman Museum SE23

www.horniman.ac.uk

100 London Rd (020) 8699 1872 1–4D

"Free Museum" is carved in stone at the entrance of this fascinating Forest Hill museum (adjacent to delightful, very well maintained gardens which boast a bandstand and lovely views over London). A visit here has something for everyone. The building grew out of the enthusiasms of Victorian tea magnate Frederick Horniman, who in 1897 opened this art nouveau gallery to house his collection. It is divided into three main collections – natural history, music and world cultures (ethnography) – and contains some 350,000 objects, as well as an aquarium. There is also an education handling collection which has over 3,700 objects taken from the collections. There is a good programme of talks and workshops in the museum, arts and crafts every Sat for children and music in the bandstand in the summer. The museum has undergone a major refurbishment and extension in recent years.
/ Times: 10.30am-5.30pm daily; BR: Forest Hill.

Imperial War Museum SE1

www.iwm.org.uk

Lambeth Rd (020) 7416 5320,

recorded information (0900) 1600140 2–4D

Despite its macho image – which the guns outside the entrance do nothing to dispel – this venue puts on a huge variety of displays offering something of interest for everyone. The heart of the collection, of course, is the fine collection of planes, tanks and every imaginable weapon of war. Using interactive video technology, however, the museum also stages some spectacular exhibits, including reconstructions such as the World War I Trench and WWII Blitz Experiences, complete with sounds and smells. Much of the material goes far beyond the 'hardware' of war, with some exhibits telling the human side of the story (which is, for practical purposes, often largely indistinguishable from the social history of the period concerned). The VCGC (Victoria Cross, George Cross) Gallery, for example, displays an array of medals and relates the stories of the people who won them. There's also a permanent Holocaust exhibition. The museum presents a fine array of exhibitions geared towards children, some enlivened by actors portraying soldiers and other historical characters. The grounds in which the museum stands – Geraldine Mary Harmsworth Park – are also home to the Tibetan Peace Garden (see also).
/ Times: 10am-6pm daily; Tube: Lambeth North, Elephant & Castle; Café.

Jerwood Space SE1
www.jerwoodspace.co.uk
171 Union St   (020) 7654 0171   5–4B
Originally a Victorian school building, this 2,600 square foot art gallery hosts a year-round exhibition programme of one-person and thematic group exhibitions. The gallery is made up of three interconnected spaces and an adjacent outdoor Sculpture Space, and is home to the esteemed Jerwood Painting Prize.
/ Times: Mon-Fri 10am-5pm, Sat-Sun 10am-3pm (recommended to call in advance on weekends as they are often closed); Tube: London Bridge, Southwark; Café, Restaurant.

Little Holland House
www.sutton.gov.uk
40 Beeches Ave, Carshalton   (020) 8770 4781
The Grade II listed interior is one of the attractions of this former home of artist, designer and craftsman Frank Dickinson (1874-1961). Wanting to create a house that would meet with the approval of his mentors, John Ruskin and William Morris, he designed and built the house and contents (in the Arts and Crafts style) himself. It took two years and was finished in 1904. Highlights include the painted frieze in the master bedroom, the carved timbers of the living room and the decorated fireplace surrounds. / Times: 1st Sun of month, bank hol Sun and Mon (except in Jan) 1.30pm-5.30pm; BR: Carshalton Beeches.

London Glassblowing SE1
www.londonglassblowing.co.uk
7 Leathermarket, Weston St   (020) 7403 2800   5–4C
The Glass Art Gallery at this well-established glass-blowing studio has three special glass-blowing exhibitions each year, as well as two exhibitions in other media. Additionally, you are welcome to watch the molten glass being blown and transformed into beautiful objects. If you so wish, you can, of course, purchase an example on the way out. There are three open weekends a year, in spring, summer and at Christmas – call for dates. / Times: Mon-Fri 10am-5pm; Tube: London Bridge, Borough; Café.

Merton Heritage Centre, Surrey
www.merton.gov.uk
The Canons, Madeira Rd, Mitcham   (020) 8640 9387
Located in a c17 mansion house in Mitcham, the centre tells the story of the borough of Merton and its people, past and present. There is a changing programme of exhibitions and special events – a past exhibition was entitled 'The Glories and the Dispossessed'. Displays usually include photographic material, artefacts, videos and a 'hands-on' section. / Times: Tue and Wed 10am-4pm, Fri and Sat 10am-4.30pm; Tube: Colliers Wood (then 200 or 152 bus), Morden (then 118 bus to Vestry Hall), Wimbledon (then 200 bus); Tramlink: Mitcham, Mitcham Junction; Café.

Mounted Police Museum
www.met.police.uk
Mounted Training Establishment, Imber Court, East
Molesey (020) 8247 5480
*Horses are trained here for public duty and ceremonies. To get
to the museum you pass through the stables themselves – the
small collection contains artefacts relating to the mounted
branch since 1920, with paintings, documents, flags and
regalia. / Times: by written appt (groups and clubs preferred); BR: Thames
Ditton.*

National Archives TW9
www.pro.gov.uk
Ruskin Ave, Kew, Richmond (020) 8876 3444 1–3A
*This is the national archive of England and Wales – 96 miles of
shelving holding records created or acquired by central
government and the central courts of law from the c11 until
the present day. All the public records previously held at the
original Chancery Lane PRO, are now housed at Kew, and this
is where you find, for example, the Domesday Book, Jane
Austen's will and Guy Fawkes's confessions. There are also
temporary exhibitions. / Times: Mon and Fri 9am-5pm, Tue and Thu
9am-7pm, Wed 10am-5pm, Sat 9.30am-5pm; BR: Kew Bridge; Tube: Kew
Gardens.*

Old Royal Naval College SE10
www.oldroyalnavalcollege.org
King William Walk (020) 8269 4791 1–3D
*Wren's baroque Greenwich Hospital (for retired sailors)
became the Royal Naval College in 1873. The extraordinary
Painted Hall (whose entire interior is decorated with paintings
by Sir James Thornhill) should particularly not be missed. The
attractive c18 chapel (decorated by James 'Athenian' Stuart) is
also worth a visit. (Services, to which all are welcome, are held
in the chapel every Sun at 11am.) The Greenwich Gateway
Visitors Centre, at the entrance to the College, contains a series
of exhibitions related to maritime Greenwich, Tudor Greenwich
and Roman Greenwich. / Times: Painted Hall and Chapel Mon-Sun
10am-5pm, except Chapel Sun from 12.30pm; Visitor Centre 10am-5pm;
DLR: Cutty Sark Gardens.*

Oxo Tower SE1
www.coinstreet.org
Bargehouse St (020) 7021 1600 5–3A
*The free public viewing platform on the eighth floor of this
South Bank Art Deco tower offers excellent views, especially
across the river to the City and St Paul's. The building itself is
home to the retail studios of artisans such as jewellers, artists,
furniture makers and ceramicists, as well as the gallery@oxo,
which often has photographic exhibitions. The nearby Bernie
Spain Gardens make a good place for children to let off steam
– you could picnic here or on the benches on the Thames-side
promenade between here and the Royal Festival Hall.
/ Times: studios Tue-Sun 11am-6pm, gallery@oxo Mon-Sun 11am-6pm;
Tube: Waterloo, Blackfriars, Southwark; Café.*

Photofusion SW9

www.photofusion.org

17A Electric Ln (020) 7738 5774 1–4C

*This Brixton gallery has bi-monthly shows by leading
international photographers. / Times: Tue-Sat 10am-6pm; Tube: Brixton.*

Pumphouse Educational Museum SE16

www.thepumphouse.org.uk

Lavender Pond Nature Park, Lavender Rd

(020) 7231 2976 1–3D

*This building, formerly housing docks machinery, is now home
to the Rotherhithe Heritage Museum and is surrounded by a
nature park. The museum traces the story of Rotherhithe and
its people, as told by objects found on the foreshore of the
Thames during 12 years beachcombing by local man, Ron
Goode. Objects include coins, clay pipes and dockers' tools.
Donations are encouraged. The Nature Park has trails through
an orchard, herb gardens and past the 'minibeast city'. Reed
beds fringe a pond which is frequented by herons, swans,
tufted ducks and dragonflies. / Times: Mon-Fri 9.30am-3.30pm;
Tube: Rotherhithe, Surrey Quays, Canada Water (from latter 2, take a 381
bus).*

Royal British Legion Poppy Factory, Surrey

www.poppyfactory.org

20 Petersham Rd, Richmond (020) 8940 3305 1–4A

*Each year around 34 million poppies are made here, as is the
wreath the Queen lays at the Cenotaph on Remembrance Sun.
The factory was set up in 1922, originally in south east
London, to help ex-members of the armed forces who are
disabled but who can work to continue to be gainfully
employed. Individuals and groups are welcome to join a tour
around this working factory. / Times: by appt tours Mon-Thu starting at
10.30am and at 1.30pm; Tube: Richmond; Restaurant.*

Royal Festival Hall* SE1

www.southbankcentre.co.uk

South Bank (087) 1663 2501 2–3D

*An iconic post-War building, the Royal Festival Hall reopened in
2007 after an extensive refurbishment. The view across the
Thames from the upper terrace of the RFH is one of the finest
in London, especially as the sun goes down. In addition, the
concert hall at the centre of Europe's largest cultural complex
offers an extensive range of free foyer events (all of which are
set out in the centre's monthly programme, and online).*

*Southbank Centre regularly hosts free events, performances
and exhibitions across the site. Enjoy live music during
lunchtime on Fri in the Central Bar or Fri evenings. The Sun
choral each week features performances of a wide range of*

music from singers, choirs and ensembles. Visit the website for more information.

While you're visiting the centre, you can take in one of the ever-changing art exhibitions in the neighbouring Festival Hall Galleries, which are open all day and evening. / *Times: 10am-11pm daily; Tube: Embankment, Waterloo; Café.*

Royal National Theatre* SE1

www.nationaltheatre.org.uk
South Bank   (020) 7452 3400   2–3D
Its uncompromising exterior may have taken a while to win Londoners' affections, but the interior of Sir Denys Lasdun's riverside building has always found favour with theatre-goers. Even if you're not going to a show, you can still explore the various levels of the intriguing layout and view one or more of the several art exhibitions, which are open all day Mon-Sat. Or take in the music – it might be early or contemporary, classical, folk or jazz – before evening and matinee performances on Sat. There's also a summer fiesta of free outdoor theatre, music and entertainment called 'Watch This Space'.
/ *Times: Mon-Sat 10am-11pm; Tube: Embankment, Waterloo; Café, Restaurant, Picnic area.*

Royal Pharmaceutical Society Museum SE1

www.rpsgb.org.uk
1 Lambeth High St   (020) 7735 7629   2–4D
The Society's museum collection has been developing since 1842 and now has approximately 45,000 items. It includes drug storage containers, medicines dating from the 1700s and a photo archive. The ground floor which is open Mon-Fri has displays such as "Lambeth's Pharmacy Past" and "Pharmacy and Nature." There is also a changing display which examines three difference medical conditions each year. The mezzanine and first floors can be visited by guided tour every Fri afternoon at 2pm and 4pm (by prior booking). These floors have an exhibition examining the past 1,000 years of pharmacy history, and includes a collection of English Delftware drug jars.
/ *Times: ground floor open Mon-Fri 9am-5pm; mezzanine and 1st floors by pre-booked guided tour Fri 2pm and 4pm.; Tube: Vauxhall.*

Shirley Windmill

www.croydononline.org
Upper Shirley Rd, Croydon   (020) 8654 0899
This five-storey brick tower mill was built in 1859, and last worked in 1892. It was restored in 1998, and retains skeleton sails, its fantail and a Kentish cap. (Note that due to the number and steepness of the stairs the mill is not suitable for the very young or for those who are less than fit.) / *Times: Jun-Oct 1st Sun in month, 1pm-5pm; BR: East Croydon (then 130 bus); Café.*

South London Art Gallery SE5

www.southlondongallery.org
65 Peckham Rd   (020) 7703 6120   1–3D
*This elegant Victorian gallery shares its site with the celebrated
Camberwell College of Arts. It presents a changing programme
of innovative contemporary works by international artists,
including a lot of 3D work, and performance art too.*
/ Times: Tue-Sun Midday-6pm during exhibition dates; BR: Peckham Rye, or 36
bus from Victoria, or 12,171 or P3 bus from Elephant & Castle.

Southwark Cathedral SE1

www.dswark.org/cathedral
Montague Close   (020) 7367 6700   5–4C
*In origin c13 (but with many later alterations), this fine
building, just over London Bridge, is something of a hidden gem.
Being rather overshadowed by the fame of the cathedrals on
the other side of the river, it benefits from an absence of
crowds. It is, in fact, the oldest Gothic church in London (and
was apparently the inspiration for Westminster Abbey). Nor
does it want for historical associations – the Bard's brother,
Edmund Shakespeare, was buried here in 1607, and that
same year saw the baptism of John Harvard, later of university
fame. At 1.10pm you may hear an organ recital (Mon) and an
instrumental music recital (Tue).* / Times: Mon-Sat 9am-6pm, Sun
9am-4pm; Tube: London Bridge; Café.

Tate Modern SE1

www.tate.org.uk
Bankside   (020) 7887 8000,
recorded information (020) 7887 8008   5–3B
*With over 4,000 paintings and 1,300 sculptures, this former
power station on the South Bank houses one of the world's
largest collections of modern art. Being free to enter (unlike,
most obviously, MoMa in New York), it has also established
itself as the most-visited modern art gallery in the world.*

*The strength of the permanent collection – very clearly eclipsed
by MoMa's – is not, however, the main reason for the gallery's
success. This probably has as much to do with the striking, and
now iconic, conversion of the former Bankside Power Station,
transformed into Tate Modern by the Swiss architects Herzog
& de Meuron. The Turbine Hall, running the length of the huge
building, provides a dramatic and gaping entrance to the
gallery. Sir Giles Gilbert Scott (who also famously designed the
red telephone box) was the architect of the original building
(completed in 1963 and decommissioned in 1981). The new
two-storey glass roof at the top of the building allows stunning
views of the City from the viewing gallery and café. The top of
the chimney is illuminated by the 'Swiss Light'.*

*The collection itself dates from 1900 onwards and, instead of
being presented chronologically, is shown in four themed*

groups: *Nude/Action/Body, History/Memory/Society, Still Life/Object/Real Life* and *Landscape/Matter/Environment. The collection includes important works by Picasso, Matisse, Dalí, Rothko and Warhol as well as contemporary work by artists such as Susan Hiller, Dorothy Cross and Gilbert & George. / Times: 10am-6pm daily (Fri and Sat 10pm) ; Tube: Southwark, Blackfriars; Café, Restaurant.*

Wimbledon Society's Museum of Local History SW19
www.wimbledonmuseum.org.uk
22 Ridgway   (020) 8296 9914   1–4B
This small, voluntarily-run museum depicts the history of Wimbledon from prehistory to the present day and includes archive material. Until recently, of course, Wimbledon was at a good remove from the metropolis, and its rural past is well illustrated by the collection of watercolours, photographs and prints. Highlights are scale models of local manor houses which no longer exist. / Times: Sat and Sun 2.30pm-5pm; Tube: Wimbledon, Putney Bridge (then 93 bus).

Winchester Palace SE1
www.english-heritage.org.uk
corner of Clink St & Storey St   5–4C
The c13 town house of the Bishops of Winchester was damaged by fire in 1814, but the remains of some of the walls of the Great Hall, with its unique rose window, still make an impressive ruin today. / Tube: London Bridge.

Outdoor attractions

Battersea Park SW11
www.wandsworth.gov.uk
Albert Bridge Rd   (020) 8871 7530   3–4D
This 200-acre park is one of the most popular and most central family destinations, and rightly so as it's full of things to look at and do. It is also the only park in central(ish) London to benefit from a position right by the Thames. The long river frontage (punctuated by the Peace Pagoda given to the people of London in 1985 by a Japanese Buddhist order) has lovely views across the river to Chelsea and the Royal Hospital. Other attractions include the Pump House art gallery, a herb garden and London's largest adventure playground for 5 to 16 year olds. Excellent literature is available from the Park Office (to the left of the Albert Bridge entrance), including 'Introducing Battersea Park' which has a map, and well-produced tree and nature trail brochures. There is also a small children's zoo (for which there is a charge). / Times: dawn-dusk; Tube: Sloane Square (then 19 or 137 bus); Café.

Beckenham Place Park BR3

www.lewisham.gov.uk
Beckenham Hill Rd   (020) 8318 3986
Woodland and meadows with walking paths that form part of the 'Green Chain' (see also). There's also a kite-flying slope and sports facilities (golf course, putting green and tennis courts). / Times: 8am-dusk; BR: Ravensbourne, Beckenham Hill.

Belair Park SE21

www.southwark.gov.uk
Gallery Rd   (020) 7525 1050   1–4C
Neighbour to Dulwich Park, Belair Park, of 30 acres, is relatively little known, but worth looking at, having been laid out in the late c18 in the classic English landscape style. You can combine a visit with a trip to the Horniman Museum (see also). / Times: 8am-dusk; BR: West Dulwich; Restaurant, Picnic area.

Bermondsey Antiques Market SE1

www.bermondseysquare.co.uk
Bermondsey Sq   1–3C
If you arrive at dawn, you'll have missed the best bargains at London's largest antiques market (so take a torch and dress warmly). As the sun rises, the professionals depart and the trippers take over. / Times: Fri 5am-midday; Tube: Night buses N53 (from Trafalgar Square), or later Borough or Elephant & Castle; Café.

Blackheath SE3

www.blackheath.org
1–4D
For centuries the heath was wild and a popular haunt for highwaymen. Now, this large, flat expanse of grass separates the pretty village of Blackheath from Greenwich Park. There are a couple of ponds (one for boating), but generally its attraction is as a big, open space for running about on. A visit here would combine well with one to the Age Exchange Reminiscence Centre (see also). / BR: Blackheath.

Brixton Market SW9

www.brixtonmarket.net
Brixton Station Rd   1–4C
In a warren of streets and alleys around Brixton tube, this is one of the most atmospheric places in London. Indeed, with its mounds of food and fabrics from Africa and the Caribbean (as well as the mundane items you might expect to find anywhere), it is arguably the place in our capital to which the tag 'exotic' can most realistically be applied. / Times: Mon-Sat 8am-5.30pm (Wed 1pm); Tube: Brixton; Café.

Chumleigh Gardens SE5

www.southwark.gov.uk
Chumleigh St, Burgess Park   (020) 7525 1050   1–3C
Tucked away, behind high walls in the bland expanses of Burgess Park is a collection of erstwhile almshouses (from 1821) and a multi-cultural garden. The garden is divided into

areas: Afro-Caribbean, English, Islamic, Mediterranean and Oriental, and all flora are labelled. There are also two ponds. Owing to the water, and the poisonous or spiny nature of some of the plants, kids should not be allowed to explore unaccompanied. / *Times: 8am-dusk (winter till 4.30pm); Tube: Elephant & Castle (then P3, 185, 176 or 40 bus); BR:Denmark Hill (then 42 bus); Café, Picnic area.*

Crystal Palace Park SE20
www.crystalpalacepark.org
Sydenham   (020) 8778 7148
The Crystal Palace was an enormous glasshouse which served as a hall at the Great Exhibition (held in Hyde Park in 1851) before being dismantled and moved to Norwood, where it was consumed by fire in 1936. There's a small museum about it (see also). However, there is much more to this large and attractive park than historical associations. The permanent free attractions include a maze, a children's play area and a unique collection of full-scale Victorian models of dinosaurs. Regular events include the annual Victorian Day (usually the last weekend in June). Over the May Day bank holiday there is also an annual vintage car rally. During the Easter and summer school holidays there are special events for kids, some of which are free. Year-round you can follow the Tree Trail – details about this and other events can be obtained from the Information Centre (at the Penge entrance). / *Times: 7.30am-dusk; information centre 9am-5pm; BR: Crystal Palace.*

Danson Park DA6
www.bexley.gov.uk
Danson Rd, Welling   (020) 8304 2631
The park, landscaped in the style of 'Capability' Brown, features an ornamental seven-hectare lake, and lends itself to a wide range of recreational activities, particularly on the lake. In the summer, boat races are a popular spectacle, and in July there is a festival and a series of outdoor concerts. The park surrounds the c18 Danson Mansion, which was designed by Sir Robert Taylor, architect of the first Bank of England. / *Times: Mon-Fri 7.30am-dusk (Nov-Jan 4.30pm), Sat and Sun 9am; BR: Bexley Heath, Welling; Café.*

Dulwich Park SE21
www.southwark.gov.uk
College Rd   (020) 8693 8635   1–4C
A fine collection of trees is the particular attraction of this pretty 75-acre Victorian park. The rhododendrons and azaleas are a beautiful feature – for these, May is the time to visit. There is also rowing on the lake during the summer months. You can combine a visit with a trip to the Horniman Museum (see also). / *Times: 8am-dusk; BR: North or West Dulwich; Café, Picnic area.*

Foots Cray Meadows

www.bexley.gov.uk
Bexley   (020) 8303 7777
This rural area of woodland and open parkland (landscaped by 'Capability' Brown) follows the course of the River Cray, and is home to an abundance of wildlife – bird-watchers often visit in the hope of seeing kingfishers. There is a bridle path and the remains of Foots Cray Place, a Palladian mansion built in 1756, but destroyed by fire in 1949. Five Archers Bridge, across the Cray, is also worth a look. / Times: 9am-3.45pm daily during winter, 9am-dusk daily during summer; BR: Bexley Heath, Welling.

Green Chain Walk

www.greenchain.com
(020) 8921 5028
The Green Chain Walk is a 40-mile network of fully signposted footpaths linking together nearly 300 parks and open spaces in SE London. Starting from three points on the River Thames, the footpaths are a twisting network threading their way through parks, commons and working farms ending at Crystal Palace Park. The network allows plenty of opportunities for choosing circular walks or following a linear route and using public transport to return to your start point. The Walk is signposted from 22 nearby railway stations and served by numerous bus routes. The website is very informative. Not least, it allows you to print off ten different leaflets, each of them telling you everything you need to know to enjoy the respective suggested walks.

Greenwich Markets SE10

www.greenwichmarket.net
(020) 8293 3110   1–3D
If you enjoy nosing around market stalls, it's well worth making a special weekend journey to Greenwich, which has what is possibly the most comprehensive – as well as the most attractively situated – series of marketplaces in London. The individual markets are: the Antiques Market, Greenwich High Road; the Open Air food market; Village Market, Stockwell Street; and the Craft Market – the original market (1837), formerly a collection of fruit and veg stalls but now selling arts and crafts. The Open Air Food Market, located at the side of the National Westminster Bank, sells home-baked breads and hot foods. / Times: Wed-Sun (check website for detailed opening times of different market areas); BR: Greenwich; Café.

Greenwich Park SE10

www.royalparks.gov.uk
Park Office, Charlton Way, Greenwich
(020) 8858 2608   1–3D
These 183 acres, enclosed in 1433, constitute the oldest of London's Royal Parks. It was popular with Henry VIII, who was born locally and who held jousting tournaments here every year. It is one of the best outdoor venues, still offering something to entertain all the family. There are red and fallow deer in the deer park (established here in the c15), flower gardens and a children's playground. Brass bands play at the

bandstand on Sun afternoons and evenings during the summer
– picnicking by the audience is encouraged. In May and July,
there are family events. There is also a free summer football
school during school holidays (Charlton Football Club, tel 020
8850 2866). The view from the top of the hill by the Old Royal
Observatory (see also) is quite something, and don't miss the
Information Centre (at the St Mary's Gate entrance) which has
rooms explaining the history and wildlife of the park. You can
find out about summer events on the website. / Times: open 6am
for pedestrians (7am for traffic); closing time varies seasonally; DLR: Cutty Sark,
Greenwich; Café, Picnic area.

Lesnes Abbey Woods
www.bexley.gov.uk
Abbey Rd, Belvedere   (020) 8312 9717
Taking its name from the c12 abbey whose remains still stand,
this 200-acre wood, together with the adjoining Bostall Heath
and woods (160 acres), makes up one of the largest areas of
trees in south London. The spring sees a tremendous show of
wild daffodils, and then wood anemones and bluebells. A rather
unusual attraction is the natural fossil bed, in which the public
can search for shark and ray teeth, and shells. The woods are
quite hilly, and it's a good idea to take stout footwear. An
information centre has been added adjacent to the ruins, and
from here, you can pick up literature on self-guided trails.
/ Times: 9am-3.45pm daily during winter, 9am-dusk daily during summer;
BR: Abbey Wood.

London Wildlife Trust Centre for Wildlife
Gardening SE15
www.wildlondon.org.uk
28 Marsden Rd   (020) 7252 9186   1–4D
For those looking for special gardening secrets – making an
area attractive to butterflies or how to cover a wall in ivy – this
is the place to go. The centre offers assistance with all matters
of natural, wildlife gardening. For extensive help, workshops
take place regularly. / Times: Tue-Thu and Sun 10.30am-4.30pm;
BR: East Dulwich, Peckham Rye.

Morden Hall Park, Surrey
www.nationaltrust.org.uk
Morden Hall Rd   (020) 8545 6850
This informal 125-acre park, owned by the National Trust, was
laid out around 1860 as a deer park. It is given additional
interest by a complex network of waterways coming off the
River Wandle (which was designed partly to be ornamental and
partly to power the snuff mills which still stand), as well as the
two-acre rose garden which boasts 2,000 rose bushes. You can
also visit the three craft workshops, and watch local artists and
artisans at work. For details of family activities, call the number
given. / Times: dawn-6pm; craft workshops 10am-5pm daily except Tue;
Tube: Morden; Café.

South London

New Covent Garden Market SW8
www.cgma.gov.uk
Nine Elms Ln   (020) 7720 2211   1–3C
Since 1974, this famous market has traded on a large and unlovely Vauxhall site which shows little sign of its origins in the charming central Georgian landmark. With over 250 companies on site, it's one of the largest wholesale markets in the UK. It's best known amongst the public as a place to buy flowers, but you can also spectate on the substantial trade in fruit and veg, and catering supplies. NB Arrive on foot for free entry. Cars are charged. / Times: Mon-Fri 3am-11am, Sat 4am-10am; Tube, BR, Bus: Vauxhall.

Nunhead Cemetery SE15
www.fonc.org.uk
Linden Rd   (020) 7732 9535   1–4D
The second-largest Victorian cemetery in London, Nunhead was first opened in 1840. It is no longer used for burials (except in the eco-friendly 'woodland burial' area.) Restoration in 2001 rescued 50 memorials as well as Thomas Little's beautiful Anglican chapel. Part of the grounds (which boast impressive views over London) now form a nature reserve, supporting a diverse range of flora and fauna (16 species of butterfly have been found). Free tours of the cemetery are conducted on the last Sun of each month (starting from the Linden Grove gates at 2.15pm), and there is also an annual open day in early summer.

On the first Sun of every month, you can join in the cemetery's ongoing conservation – tea and biscuits are provided to volunteers (who must be a member of the Friends, which costs £2 a year). Activities might include pruning, pond building or inscription recording – see the website for more details. / Times: 8.30am-7pm daily (Oct 1-Mar 31 closes one hour before sunset daily) BR: Nunhead.

Old Royal Observatory* SE10
www.rog.nmm.ac.uk
Greenwich Park   (020) 8858 4422   1–3D
At the top of the hill in Greenwich Park, this charming c17 observatory has one of London's few surviving Wren interiors. The main attraction, of course, is to visit the 0 degrees longitude line – many people consider that being photographed with one foot in the western hemisphere, and the other in the eastern, is an obligatory souvenir.

The observatory is the spiritual home of the Greenwich Time Signal (though the actual electronic clocks are now kept elsewhere). A longer-established, and visual, sign of time passing is the red ball on top of the Observatory, which descends its pole at 1pm every day. The original purpose was to enable seafarers to set their chronometers correctly, which was essential if they were to be able to locate themselves, by reference to the stars, on long sea journeys.

The view from outside the Observatory is possibly the best in London and also summarises the history of the city. Immediately ahead, you see the city's imperial past (the Royal Naval College), to the west sprawls the City and central London, and across the river looms the future (or at least what until very recently seemed likely to be the future), in the form of the burgeoning towers of Canary Wharf. / Times: dawn-dusk; DLR: Greenwich.

Oxleas Woods SE18
www.greenwich.gov.uk
Shooters Hill, Eltham   (020) 8854 8888
One of the capital's last remaining ancient woodlands (some 8,000 years old) was saved from the road-builder's bulldozer in the late-1980s. The wood supports over 33 different species of tree and shrub, including the rare wild service tree, the hornbeam and guelder rose. Fungi proliferate, with more than 200 species, including the 'storybook' toadstool, the poisonous fly agaric (red with white spots). Worth a glance is Sevendroog Castle, a folly that was built as a memorial to Sir William James Bart in the 1780s. The wood forms part of the Green Chain Walk (see also). There is parking within the woods, accessible from Shooters Hill (A207) and some of the other surrounding roads. / BR: Falconwood; Café, Picnic area.

Richmond Park
www.royalparks.gov.uk
Holly Lodge, Richmond (office address)
(020) 8948 3209   1–4A
This enormous park (some four square miles) was created by Charles I by enclosing farmlands, and was used for hunting. Some remains of Richmond Palace – the gateway on the Green and the restored Wardrobe buildings – can still be seen. The park has changed little in the last 300 years, and still contains some 700 red and fallow deer. Because it has been disturbed very little, the park offers some rare natural habitats and has been declared a Site of Special Scientific Interest and, since 2000, a National Nature Reserve. The Isabella Plantation (towards the Kingston Gate) is noted for its fabulous collection of azaleas, and views from King Henry's Mound (which may have been a Bronze Age burial 'barrow') stretch as far as the City. / Times: 7am (summer), 7.30am (winter)-dusk ; Tube: Richmond.

Surrey Docks Farm SE16
www.surreydocksfarm.org.uk
Rotherhithe St   (020) 7231 1010   1–3D
This well-equipped city farm is in a slightly away-from-it-all and picturesque location, on the banks of the Thames opposite Canary Wharf. In addition to all the usual animals, attractions include an orchard, a blacksmith's forge, a nomadic Mongolian felt tent, a herb garden, vegetable gardens and beehives – it is possible in the autumn for kids to help collect the honey. Family visits are free but there is a charge for groups. / Times: Tue-Sun 10am-5pm; Tube: Rotherhithe; Café.

Sydenham Hill Wood Local Nature Reserve SE26
www.wildlondon.org.uk
Crescent Wood Rd   (020) 8699 5698   1–4D
This preserve of rare and ancient woodlands, some more than 400 years old, faced imminent destruction before the London Wildlife Trust took control in 1982. The area covers over 50 acres and is home to some 200 species of wildflowers and trees, as well as over 50 species of birds and mammals. The preserve also includes relics of an impressive Victorian garden, a remnant of a c19 estate. / Times: 24 hours; BR: Sydenham Hill.

Thames Barrier* SE18
www.greenwich.gov.uk
1 Unity Way   (020) 8854 1373
The Thames Barrier is the largest movable anti-flooding protection device in the world – it was built in response to the ever-greater threat posed to low-lying central London by high tides (which have been rising at the rate of about 75cm a century). The barrier spans the 520m Woolwich Reach and consists of 10 separate, massive, movable steel gates. The most spectacular time to visit is during the annual all-day test (in September or October), when the entire barrier blocks the high tide, but it's an impressive sight at any time. (There are also monthly closures, but these happen as early in the morning as possible to minimise closure of the river.) There is a charge for the visitors centre, but not for access to the riverside walk or the children's play area. / Times: Mon-Fri 10am-5pm, Sat and Sun 10.30am-5.30pm; BR: Charlton.

Tibetan Peace Garden SE1
www.tibet-foundation.org
St George's Rd
(020) 7930 6001 (Tibet Foundation)   2–4D
This charming garden, situated in a park shared by the Imperial War Museum (see also), was dedicated in 1999 by the Dalai Lama. The centrepiece is the language pillar, containing a message of peace in four languages – Tibetan, English, Hindi and Chinese. The garden's design incorporates the fundamental Buddhist image, the Wheel of Dharma, and contains sculptures, a bronze cast and native Himalayan and Tibetan plants. / Times: 24 hours; Tube: Lambeth North, Elephant & Castle.

Tower Bridge* SE1
www.towerbridge.org.uk
(020) 7403 3761   5–4D
One of London's great symbols, the bridge was built between 1886 and 1894. Despite its appearance, it is, in fact, a thoroughly modern steel structure, but was clad in stone to harmonise with the Tower of London. The halves of the bridge (originally steam-powered, but now electrically operated) can still be raised to accommodate large vessels needing access to the Pool of London – the website gives a schedule of forthcoming lifts. There is a fascinating display inside the bridge which explains the workings of the original machinery, but for this there is sadly a charge. / Tube: Tower Hill.

Vauxhall City Farm SE11

www.vauxhallcityfarm.info

24 St Oswald's Place   (020) 7582 4204   1–3C

It may be less than an acre in size, but this tiny farm, run on a voluntary basis, boasts a full range of farm animals. Look out for rabbits, geese, ponies, donkeys and sheep. There is also an ecology garden and some allotments. Spinning and weaving groups. / Times: Wed-Sun 10.30am-4pm Seasonal closures-call in advance to confirm; Tube: Vauxhall; Picnic area (sometimes, Sun 14.00-16.00).

Well Hall Pleasaunce SE9

www.greenwich.gov.uk

Well Hall Rd, Eltham   (020) 8856 2232

A rose garden, a stream and a waterfall, as well as a moat and colourful flowerbeds are among the features of this unusual park, surrounding a c15 Tudor barn (now a café). / ; Café.

Wimbledon Common SW19

www.wpcc.org.uk

(020) 8788 7655   1–4B

The common – as older readers will know, home to the Wombles, who keep it clear of rubbish – extends to nearly two square miles, some of which is quite rough countryside, and there are several ponds with much birdlife. It is the setting for one of London's few remaining windmills, which now houses a museum (Apr-Oct) about the history of this type of machinery, complete with working models, for which there is a charge, albeit a small one. A new addition is a wheelchair track, on the nature trail, that allows those on wheels to cover part of the common. This trail also includes sign posts bearing nature information. / Times: pedestrians 24 hours; vehicles sunrise-sunset; Tube: Southfields, Wimbledon; Café, Picnic area.

Woolwich Foot Tunnel

www.greenwich.gov.uk

North Woolwich Pier, New Ferry Approach

(020) 8854 8888 ext 5493 (to confirm lift times)

Another chance to walk under the Thames (see also Greenwich Foot Tunnel) which combines nicely with a trip over the river, on the Woolwich Free Ferry (see also). / Times: lift service, Mon-Sat 7am-7pm, Sun 10am-5.30pm; BR: north of the Thames, North Woolwich; south of the Thames, Woolwich Arsenal, Woolwich Dockyard, or 180 bus to Greenwich.

Woolwich Free Ferry SE18

www.greenwich.gov.uk

North Woolwich Pier, New Ferry Approach

(020) 8921 5786

The ferry – the only free automated way to cross the Thames – began in 1889. Paddlesteamers were, alas, replaced by the current, less romantic, design in 1963. / Times: Mon-Sat 6.10am-8pm Sun 11.30am-7.30pm; BR: north of the Thames, North Woolwich; south of the Thames Woolwich Arsenal, Woolwich Dockyard.

The City

Introduction

The tiny, but very wealthy Square Mile is often likened to a city-state. It has its own ways of doing things which have been arrived at over practically a millennium of running its own affairs, and its long history has left it rich in historic buildings and institutions. Its wealth and importance are symbolised by its medieval **Guildhall**, where great banquets for foreign heads of state are held, and by the great cathedral of St Paul's – other great sights include the **Tower of London**, **Tower Bridge** and the **Monument**.

Trading and, later, banking were the foundations of the City's wealth. Today more international banks gather together in the City than anywhere else. Almost all trading and banking business nowadays happens over the telephone, or sometimes electronically without any obvious human intervention at all. For the casual visitor, the **Bank of England Museum** provides the only insight into these rather closed worlds. If you want to see institutions at work, the barristers' **Inns of Court** are some of the most interesting, picturesque and immutable of all – and most are open to the public to a greater or lesser extent.

The City also has indoor attractions such as the **Clockmakers' Company Collection** and the **London Silver Vaults** – both of which should be of interest to older children and adults.

If planning a visit, it's a good idea to arrive in the late morning and begin by visiting the City Tourist Information Office – there is usually at least one free lunchtime concert in one of the City's fine churches (many designed by Wren).

General Information

City of London Information Centre EC4
www.visitthecity.co.uk
St Paul's Churchyard   (020) 7332 1456   5–2B
The City has a conveniently positioned general tourist information centre right by St Paul's. It has copies of City Events, an excellent guide to the musical and other events happening in the City during that month. / Times: Mon-Sat 9.30am-5.30pm, Sun 10am-4pm; Tube: St Paul's.

The City and its architecture
A leaflet, available from the City of London Information Centre, lists all buildings of historical and architectural interest within the Square Mile. Opening times, maps, the nearest tube stations and suggested walking routes are included, as well as a brief history of the City and sketches of the buildings described. The churches of the City (many by Wren) are a particular architectural treasure of the capital.

Suggested walk

An afternoon walk through the City, leads one through
1,000 years of London history. Begin at Tower Bridge
and the Tower of London. Move west along Tower Street,
which becomes Eastcheap, until reaching Monument, to
learn about the Great Fire of 1666. Next, an interesting
stop would be the Bank of England Museum. Follow King
William Street north and west until it meets Threadneedle
Street. The Bank is ahead of you, and the entrance to the
museum is on Bartholomew Lane, to your right. From the
museum you have two options. One is to head south
along Queen Victoria Street until reaching St. Peter's Hill.
Descending the steps to the Thames brings you to the
foot of the Millennium footbridge, which connects the
City with the Tate Modern gallery at Southwark (see also).
Alternatively, you can head west from the Bank of England
along Cheapside to St Paul's Cathedral. From here, it's not
far to the Barbican. If you time your walk correctly –
concluding around 5.30pm – you'll be able to take in an
early evening performance in the foyer of the concert
halls.

Indoor attractions

Association of Photographers Gallery EC2
www.the-aop.org
81 Leonard St   (020) 7739 6669   5–1C
*A contemporary photographic gallery, holding around a dozen
temporary exhibitions annually.* / Times: Mon-Fri 10am-6pm, occasional
Sat noon-4pm; Tube: Old Street.

Bank of England Museum EC2
www.bankofengland.co.uk
Bartholomew Ln   (020) 7601 5545   5–2C
*A more than usually topical attraction in current times! Housed
within the forbidding building of the Bank itself, the museum is
at the very centre of the City of London and traces the history
of the Bank from its royal foundation in 1694 right up to the
present. There are four DVD interactive videos which help bring
the institution's activities to life, by telling the role of the bank
today as well as the history of bank note design and
production. The museum has gold bars and a copy of every
design of bank note the Bank has ever issued. Curiosities
include documents relating to George Washington (a former
customer), Kenneth Grahame (a former Secretary of the Bank,
as well as being the author of* The Wind in the Willows*) and
the original cartoon by James Gillray which famously satirised
the Bank as the 'Old Lady of Threadneedle Street'. The neo-
classical Bank Stock Office by Sir John Soane, recreated for the
museum, makes a graceful centrepiece and is used for
temporary exhibitions.* / Times: Mon-Fri 10am-5pm; also day of the Lord
Mayor's Show (2nd Sat in Nov, see also); Tube: Bank.

Barbican* EC2

www.barbican.org.uk

Silk St   (020) 7638 4141   5–1B

Love it or hate it, the City's sprawling, concrete arts and residential complex is undoubtedly impressive, with its vast concert hall, theatre, cinema and sweeping internal spaces – the biggest arts centre under a single roof anywhere in the world. There are FreeStage events in the foyer (anything from jazz to Irish folk music) most days between 5.30pm and 7.15pm (and also most Sun 12.30pm-2.30pm) – see the centre's programme for details – and there are often special themed events on bank holiday weekends. Free displays, often by local artists, take place in the library foyer, and there other exhibitions in the Concourse Gallery, Foyer Gallery, Craftspace and Jewellery Case. / Times: 9am (Sun noon)-11pm; library Mon-Sat 9.30am-5.30pm (Tue 7pm, Sat noon); Concourse Gallery Mon-Sun 10.30am (Sun noon)-7.30pm; bank hols noon-6pm; Tube: Barbican, Moorgate; Café.

Clerks' Well EC1

www.islington.gov.uk

14-16 Farringdon Ln   (020) 7527 7988   5–1A

The source that gave the surrounding area of Clerkenwell its name was subsequently filled in and built over. Rediscovered in 1924 the well chamber can still be visited – you can see an iron pump and plaque from 1800, some c16 refacing work and a later wall probably from the c17. Access is by key from the local library, see details below. Groups – 4 to 15 people – preferred. / Times: Mon, Tue, Thu, and Sat 10am-5pm by appt ; Tube: Farringdon, Angel, Barbican.

Clockmakers' Company Collection EC2

www.clockmakers.org

Guildhall Library, Aldermanbury   (020) 7332 1868   5–2C

The Clockmakers' Company may go back only to 1631, but its collection of clocks dates from the c14. This single-room horological museum (which has been extensively refurbished in recent times) contains a glittering and fascinating selection of timepieces including curiosities, such as the first electric clock. There is also a large silver watch reputed to have belonged to Mary Queen of Scots, and the one worn by Edmund Hillary during his ascent of Everest in 1953. To hear the collection at its best, make sure you are there at noon. / Times: Mon-Sat 9.30am-4.45pm; Tube: St Paul's, Bank, Moorgate, Mansion House .

College of Arms EC4

www.college-of-arms.gov.uk

Queen Victoria St   (020) 7248 2762   5–3B

The College, which traces its origins to the c13, is the body empowered by the sovereign to determine everything relating to the granting of new coats of arms and the right to bear arms which have been granted in the past. The main part of its building is c17, while the impressive wrought iron gates came from a country house and were given by an American benefactor. The Earl Marshal's Court Room is one of the finest secular period rooms in the City to which the public has access. / Times: Mon-Fri 10am-4pm; Tube: Blackfriars, St Pauls.

Guildhall EC1

www.cityoflondon.gov.uk
Gresham St   (020) 7606 3030   5–2C
The hall on this site has been the most important secular building in the City since the c11 – many important events and glittering state banquets take place here. Much of the present building (which is on a spectacular scale) dates from 1411, and, although fire and bomb damage have taken their toll, a fair amount of the original remains. The magnificent hall is usually open to casual visitors (ring to check), and pre-booked parties (10-50 people) may also visit the Old Library and the medieval crypt. / Times: free after 3.30pm daily and all day Fri (can close without notice so call ahead); Tube: St Paul's, Bank.

Guildhall Art Gallery EC1

www.visitthecity.co.uk
Gresham St   (020) 7332 3700   5–2C
The gallery houses the Corporation of London's collection of art, now numbering some 4000 items, which was started in the c17. Works range from portraits of monarchs to a good collection of Victorian pictures. Around 250 works of art are exhibited at any one time along with a programme of differently themed temporary exhibitions (ring or check website for details). The gallery also houses the Roman Amphitheatre which is beneath the art gallery and dates from the second-century AD. / Times: 3.30pm-5pm, Fri 10am-5pm; Tube: St Paul's, Bank.

Guildhall Library EC2

www.cityoflondon.gov.uk
Aldermanbury   (020) 7332 1868   5–2C
This elegant library specialises in the history of London. If this is an area which interests you, this is a delightful place to while away a couple of hours. Information not available on the shelves can normally be retrieved from the stores within 10 minutes. There is an area where visitors can consume packed lunches. Within the same building as the library, you can visit the Guildhall Clock Museum (see also). / Times: Mon-Sat 9.30am-5pm (Bookshop and Printroom closed Sat); Tube: Moorgate, Bank, St Paul's.

Islington Museum EC1

www.islington.gov.uk
245 St John St   (020) 7527 2837   4–3D
The new Islington Museum opened in 2008 underneath the Finsbury Library. It contains a gallery about Islington's history covering topics such as wartime, leisure and childhood. Its collection includes unique items such as a bust of Lenin, a former resident of Clerkenwell. Frequent free exhibitions. / Times: Mon, Tue, Thu-Sat 10am-5pm; Tube: Angel.

Livery Halls EC1

www.cityoflondon.gov.uk
(020) 7332 1456
The proud and ancient livery companies of the City – originally trade guilds – boast a large number of halls, some of which are extremely grand and historic. Gaining access to most of them is

The City

difficult, but it is worth applying to the City Information Office early in each year for part of the small allocation of tickets which they receive every February. The companies participating in the scheme vary, but have recently included the Goldsmiths and the Ironmongers. The Corporation of London website (www.cityoflondon.gov.uk) has links to all the major livery company websites. Contact the City of London for more information and booking on (020) 7332 1456.

London Metropolitan Archives EC1
www.cityoflondon.gov.uk/lma
40 Northampton Rd   (020) 7332 3820   4–4D
The name says it all. For anyone interested in the history of London (and Middlesex) – or wanting to research their Londoner forebears – this City-fringe establishment offers a fascinating glimpse at city life in past centuries. There are documents, books, maps and photographs – many on open access, but some available only upon request. The earliest documents date from the c13. / Times: Mon-Fri 9.30am-4.45pm (Tue and Thu 7.30pm), selected Sat 9.30am-4.45pm (call or see website for dates); Tube: King's Cross, Farringdon, Angel; Café (1).

Museum & Library of the Order of St John* EC1
www.sja.org.uk/history
St John's Gate, St John's Ln   (020) 7324 4070   5–1A
The ground floor of St John's Gate (see also) houses the historic collections of the Order which include Maltese silver and furniture, pharmacy jars, paintings, prints, drawings and arms and armour. All items reflect the history and work of the Knights Hospitaller from the time of the Crusades to the present day St John Ambulance. An exhibition, Time to Care, *tells the story of the St John Ambulance Association (formed in 1887) which today operates in over 43 countries. The exhibition showcases stories of St John Ambulance work and includes medieval artefacts, multimedia interactive exhibits, film and oral history, as well as paintings and displays. Tours can be arranged which take in the Museum but also the rest of St John's Gate (see also). NB The museum will close for renovations at some point during the currency of this guide.* / Times: Mon-Fri 10am-5pm, Sat (library by appt, exhibition rms 10am-4pm); tours Tue, Fri, Sat 11am and 2.30pm; Tube: Farringdon; Café, Restaurant, Picnic area.

Museum of London* EC2
www.museumoflondon.org.uk
150 London Wall
(020) 7001 9844 (recorded information)   5–2B
One of London's most interesting and best-presented museums, offering permanent and temporary exhibitions revealing the history of the capital from prehistoric times to the present day. The ever-changing displays might cover anything from photographs of football fans to displays about royal fashion. Star exhibits include the spectacular gilded Lord Mayor's coach (wheeled out once a year for the eponymous Show – see also) and a genuine c18 prison cell complete with prisoners' graffiti. There is also a 'London before London' exhibition in the Pre-

History gallery, which charts the history of the area over the last ten million years and includes a thousand objects. At lunchtimes there are occasional free lectures and films.

In 2009, the museum is undergoing a major redevelopment, transforming the way it tells London's story from 1666 to the present day. The new modern London galleries will open in early-2010 but until then visitors can still visit the prehistoric, Roman and medieval London galleries, as well as events and exhibitions for all ages including London's Burning, *a special exhibition which explores the Great Fire of London.*
/ Times: Mon-Sun 10am-5.50pm; Tube: Barbican, Bank, St Paul's, Moorgate; Café.

Oak Room EC1
www.islington.gov.uk
173 Rosebery Ave   (020) 7833 9527   4–3D
By prior appointment, this c17th room, designed by Wren's protégé Grinling Gibbons, is open to the public. It was built originally as the boardroom (in modern parlance) of the New River Company (an important early scheme to bring clean water to the metropolis), and has been moved from its initial location. / Times: Mon-Fri 9am-5.30pm, by appt; Tube: Angel (or 19 or 38 buses).

Old Bailey EC4
www.oldbaileyonline.org
Newgate St   (020) 7248 3277   5–2B
The Central Criminal Court, as it is more properly called, is the site of London's most notorious trials. All human life is there, and there's usually something intriguing, amusing or just plain bizarre to listen to. If you're only paying a brief visit, the most interesting thing to do is to catch the cross-examination of a witness by a bewigged barrister. There are two public gallery entrances: Warwick Passage, off Old Bailey, and Newgate Street. Children below the age of 14 are not allowed. Those under 16 must be accompanied by an adult. / Times: Mon-Fri 10am-1pm, 2pm-4pm; Tube: St Paul's, Blackfriars.

St Etheldreda EC1
www.stetheldreda.com
14 Ely Place   (020) 7405 1061   5–2A
Britain's oldest catholic church (1250s) is the only surviving building of the Bishop of Ely's London residence, Ely House (referred to in the writings of both Shakespeare and Dickens). It has some very good Gothic architecture, as well as a good choir which can be enjoyed at Sun services. / Times: 8am-6pm daily (The Crypt Café is open weekdays noon and 2.30pm); Tube: Chancery Lane, Farringdon; Café.

Smithfield Market EC1
Smithfield   (020) 7248 3151   5–2A
There has been a meat market in Smithfield since the 1100s, though the current building – designed by the architect for Tower Bridge, Horace Jones – was built in 1868. It's an extremely atmospheric piece of design (in a characterful and increasingly trendy bit of town) and was recently repainted with

the aim of recreating the original colour scheme. To this day it is the largest meat market in London. Although the public are not allowed in every section due to health regulations, it's worth an early morning visit which can be followed by a pint and full breakfast at one of the nearby pubs, which have special dispensation to open early (7am). / Times: Mon-Fri 4am-10am (trading usually ends by 7am); Tube: Farringdon.

St Bartholomew's Museum EC1

www.bartsandthelondon.org.uk
West Smithfield   (020) 7601 8152   5–2B
Original archives, artefacts and medical instruments, together with video and sound recordings, tell the story of this famous hospital from its foundation in 1123 to the present day. Of particular interest is the Charter signed by Henry VIII preventing the closure of the hospital during the Dissolution of the Monasteries and eight sound recordings of doctors and nurses recreating their daily lives from 1500-present. Kids might particularly like the amputation kits and bleeding bowls, and the wooden head used for practising trepanning (drilling through the scalp). / Times: Tue-Fri 10am-4pm; Tube: Barbican, St Paul's; Café, Restaurant, Picnic area.

St John's Gate EC1

www.sja.org.uk/history
St John's Gate, St John's Ln   (020) 7324 4070   5–1A
Built in 1504, the Gate was the entrance to the Priory of the Knights Hospitaller and has also been variously: entrance to the office of the Master of the Revels (licensing Shakespeare's plays); a coffee house run by Hogarth's father; a club venue for Dickens, Cruikshank and other c19th notables; a tavern; and – last but not least – birthplace of St John Ambulance. Tours visit upstairs rooms in the Gate as well as the c14 Priory Church and Norman Crypt (one of the few remaining in London). / Times: Mon-Fri 10am-5pm (Sat 4pm), Tours (donations requested and groups must book) Tue, Fri, Sat 11am and 2.30pm; Tube: Farringdon.

Wesley's Chapel EC1

www.wesleyschapel.org.uk
49 City Rd   (020) 7253 2262   5–1C
John Wesley, the father of Methodism, had his chapel and house built in 1778 to the designs of George Dance the Younger. You can visit the chapel and Wesley's tomb, which are part of this fine group of Georgian buildings on the northern fringe of the City. (Wesley's House and the Museum of Methodism can also be visited during the same hours, but for these there is a charge.) / Times: Mon-Sat 10am-4pm, Sun noon -1.45pm; Tube: Old Street, Moorgate.

Outdoor attractions

Broadgate* EC2

www.broadgateinfo.net
(020) 7505 4000   5–2D
One summer (end May-beginning of Sep) lunchtime, when the weather is hot, why not visit the City's Broadgate development.

Most weekdays between 12.30pm and 2pm, this Manhattan-style complex of offices, shops and restaurants puts on musical or other entertainments (usually at some point including an unusual exhibition; in the past, for example, it has been a display of Spanish dressage with Andalucian horses). Giant chess and draughts sets are provided, too. During the winter, you could spend an evening (dress warmly) watching teams compete at broomball on London's only permanent outdoor ice-rink – or try ice-skating for yourself (there is a charge). A monthly diary of events – Broadgate Live – is available from the Arena office (or you can call to be put on the mailing list).
/ Tube: Liverpool Street.

Inns of Court
www.barcouncil.org.uk
(020) 7427 4800 (Middle Temple); (020) 7405 1393 (Lincoln's Inn); (020) 7458 7800 (Gray's Inn); (020) 7797 8177 (Inner Temple); (020) 7353 8559 (Temple Church)   5–2A
Lawyers have clustered around the City since the earliest times. Even today, every barrister practising in England and Wales must be a member of one of the four inns of court (the Middle and Inner Temples, Gray's and Lincoln's Inns). These bodies are effectively medieval colleges, with their own dining halls, libraries, gardens and chapels. They are also landlords to the barristers' chambers (offices).

All of the inns give the public access to some part of their territories, which are peaceful, charming and often of considerable antiquity.
Starting in the Temple, don't miss Middle Temple Hall, a large Tudor hall with a magnificent double hammer-beam roof. This area is also rich in historical trivia – not only was Twelfth Night first performed in the hall here by the Bard's own company (1602), but the Wars of the Roses took their name from red and white blooms plucked from the garden behind. The hall at the neighbouring Inner Temple is not open to the public (although the gardens are, noon-3pm daily), but the main sight there is the Temple Church, the only circular church in London and one of London's oldest buildings (c12).

Leaving the Temple, and progressing up Chancery Lane, you come first to Lincoln's Inn, with its fine, sweeping lawns, halls (one c15, one c19) and chapel (noon-2.30pm only), and then to Gray's Inn, whose chapel and walks (at lunchtime) are open to public view. Organised groups can see the inside of the rest of the building, including the medieval hall, by writing to the Under Treasurer, Honorable Society of Gray's Inn, Treasury Office, 8 South Square, London WC1R 5ET.

The grounds of all the inns are open on weekdays. Mid-morning and mid-afternoons of weekdays are generally the best times to gain access to the halls and chapels – if you are making a special trip, it may be wise to call to confirm access.
/ Times: Middle Temple Hall 10am-11.30am, 3pm-4pm; call for other times; all temples closed Sat and Sun; Tube: Temple, Chancery Lane.

Leadenhall Market EC3

www.leadenhallmarket.co.uk
Whittington Ave   (0871) 789 6001   5–2C
For an atmospheric City experience, there's little to rival a stroll around this quite small but atmospheric and impressive covered Victorian market (whose architect was Horace Jones, who also designed Tower Bridge and Smithfield Market). It stands in stark contrast to the new Lloyds building, which towers over it. / Times: public areas 24hrs, market stalls Wed-Fri (contact individual shops for times); Tube: Bank, Monument.

Leather Lane Market EC1

www.leatherlanemarket.co.uk
Leather Ln   5–1A
A street market for over 300 years, and still one of the most atmospheric in London. It's also relatively untouched by the tourist hand despite being in the heart of Clerkenwell, with the crush of shoppers mainly comprising locals and workers on their lunchbreak from nearby offices. The range of goods on sale covers the usual bases: from fruit and veg to plants, jewellery, clothes and household goods. / Times: Mon-Fri 10am-2.30pm; Tube: Chancery Lane.

The Monument* EC2

www.themonument.info
Monument St & Fish St Hill   5–3C
The Great Fire of 1666 swept away much of the medieval City. The burghers of the day commissioned Wren to memorialise the devastation and the Monument – still the highest free-standing stone column in the world – was the result. Its height (202 feet) is the same as its distance from the baker's shop in Pudding Lane where the fire started. The story is given in detail in the large notice at the base of the column, which emerged in 2009 from a major refurbishment. You can climb to the top, but there's a small charge. / Tube: Monument.

Postman's Park EC1

Little Britain, King Edward St   5–2B
A tiny entrance opposite the National Postal Museum leads into a small and unprepossessing park with benches and grass. However, follow the path and you see a long wooden porch protecting what looks like the rear wall of a block of flats and a slightly raised patio. Set into the wall are around 50 memorials to 'heroic men and women', many with a story to tell, and on the south side of the park is Michel Ayrton's bronze Minotaur, added in 1973. / Tube: St Paul's, Barbican.

Tower of London* EC3

www.tower-of-london.com
West Gate, Tower of London   (020) 7709 0765   5–3D
The Tower of London is one of the most interesting and historic sites in London, and unfortunately charges handsomely for entering its precincts or visiting the treasures within (which, of course, include the Crown Jewels). You can get a good perspective of the medieval building from the riverside walk, however (and see also Ceremony of the Keys). / Tube: Tower Hill.

East London

Introduction

Centuries of being the poor relation among the areas of London has left east London ('the East End') with a very different range of amenities from any other area. It means, for example, that in the inner city there is only one park of any note, **Victoria Park**. However, if you are prepared to go as far as the end of the Central Line, you will, in **Epping Forest**, find the largest medieval woodland anywhere near London. A feature of east London which is of particular interest to children is the city farms, which are quite rare elsewhere.

As regeneration of the East End 'proper' takes hold, however, some very notable attractions are springing up. Canary Wharf, the largest office development in Europe, has given the Isle of Dogs Britain's tallest building, at 50 storeys high. The redevelopment of **St Katharine Docks** has created what is by far the nicest marina in inner London – on a sunny day, it's a really charming place. The continuing efforts to improve the **Lee Valley Regional Park** are beginning to make it an amenity which offers a large range of attractions.

The area is well served with non-commercial art galleries (the refurbished **Whitechapel Art Gallery** being the grandest and longest established).

For people-watching and browsing, the area has several of London's most characterful markets – **Petticoat Lane** and **Brick Lane**, and **Columbia Road Flower Market**, which are particularly popular Sunday morning destinations, and can be joined together on an interesting stroll (especially if you take in the former Truman Brewery on Brick Lane, which has been funkily redeveloped into a series of retail and gallery spaces with cafés and bars).

A trip on the (overground) Docklands Light Railway (from Bank or Tower Hill; www.dlr.co.uk) is an ideal way to see the much of the area. Travel is free if you have a Travelcard and, at weekends, a running commentary points out all the old dock areas and London's original Chinatown at Limehouse. End your trip in Greenwich and explore (see South London).

Essex Tourist Information Centre, Essex
County Hall, Market Rd, Chelmsford   (01245) 283400
/ *Times: Mon-Sat 10am-5pm (Sat 4pm); www.essexcc.gov.uk; BR: Chelmsford.*

Redbridge Tourist Information Centre, Essex
Clements Rd, Ilford   (020) 8708 2420
/ *Times: Mon-Fri 9.30am-8pm (Sat 4pm); www.redbridge.gov.uk; BR: Ilford.*

Indoor attractions

Chisenhale Gallery E3
www.chisenhale.org.uk
64 Chisenhale Rd   (020) 8981 4518   1–2D
This contemporary gallery holds half a dozen mixed media shows a year by British and foreign artists. Many of the British artists shown here have subsequently been nominated for the prestigious Turner Prize. / Times: Wed-Sun 1pm-6pm; Tube: Mile End, Bethnal Green.

Clowns International Archives E8
www.clowns-international.co.uk
Holy Trinity Church, Beechwood Rd, Dalston
(020) 7608 0312   1–1D
Formerly called The Clowns Gallery, The Clowns Museum has moved to Somerset but the archives are still in London. The Grimaldi Corner of the church, along with displays from the collection, are open for public viewing. / Times: 1st Fri of month, noon-5pm; Tube: Liverpool St, then bus 149 or 242.

Flowers E2
www.flowerseast.com
82 Kingsland Rd   (020) 7920 7777   5–1D
An internationally recognised gallery works to establish young and new artists through their exhibitions, and mainly featuring contemporary British painters. / Times: Tue-Sat 10am-6pm; Tube: Old Street.

Geffrye Museum E2
www.geffrye-museum.org.uk
Kingsland Rd   (020) 7739 9893   1–2D
This is a rather special museum, situated in elegant early c18 almshouses, which tells the story of English domestic interiors through a series of period rooms from Elizabethan times to the 1990s. From Apr-Oct, there's also an enchanting walled herb garden and a fine display of period gardens, showing a visual history of town gardens over the past four hundred years. In summer the museum organises unusual, intelligent activities for kids and there is often music (not always period), inside or in the garden – check website for details. / Times: Tue-Sat 10am-5pm, Sun and bank hols noon-5pm; Tube: Liverpool Street, Old Street; Restaurant.

Hackney Museum E8
www.hackney.gov.uk
1 Reading Lane   (020) 8356 2509   1–1D
The museum was established in 1986 to collect and preserve evidence regarding the history of Hackney from Viking times, and moved to its current location in 2002. It boasts state-of-the-art displays, an education room and artefact stores. It's the displays that reflect the area's cultural diversity which are the particular attraction. Perhaps of special interest to local residents is 'Hackney Voices', a CD-ROM of information, photographs and interviews with first-generation Hackney residents about their experiences of settling in the borough. / Times: Tue, Wed, Fri 9.30am-5.30pm, Thu 9.30am-8pm, Sat 10am-5pm; BR: Hackney Central.

Hazle Ceramics Workshop*

www.hazle.com

33-35 Barleylands Craft Centre, Barleylands Rd

(12682) 70892

See how an award-winning range of collectable ceramic wall plaques is made. (If you decide you want to participate, there's a small charge.) / Times: 10am-5pm daily; BR: Brentwood (then 265 bus).

Island History Trust E14

www.islandhistory.org.uk

Docklands Settlement, 197 East Ferry Rd

(020) 7987 6041   1–3D

The Trust documents the social history of the Isle of Dogs, an area which has, in turn, seen massive industrial growth, severe bomb damage, recession and, most recently, large-scale urban renewal. Five thousand pictures – from the 1870s to the 1960s – show street scenes, churches, sport, work, social lives, pubs and families. All are captioned and indexed and so of particular interest to people who have a connection with the area, or who wish to research family history. The area is named after a small island in the Thames which has long since disappeared – the site itself was never an island. / Times: Tue, Wed, and 1st Sun of every month 1.30pm-4.30pm; Tube: Island Gardens (DLR), Mudchute (DLR); Café, Restaurant, Picnic area.

London Ambulance Service Museum

www.londonambulance.nhs.uk

North East Sector HQ, Aldborough Rd South, Ilford

(020) 8557 1767

The museum's collection includes more than 20 vehicles – ranging from the horse-drawn ambulance of 1870 to a paramedic motorcycle of 1991. There is, however, much emphasis on the human aspects of the ambulance service, with curiosities including a first aid box that belonged to Prince Albert. / Times: by appt Mon-Fri 9.30am-4pm; Tube: Newbury Park.

Matt's Gallery E3

www.mattsgallery.org

42-44 Copperfield Rd   (020) 8983 1771   1–2D

This contemporary gallery commissions works ranging from installations which are made in – and specifically for – the space, to video, photography and painting exhibitions. Check website for details of exhibitions. / Times: Wed-Sun noon-6pm (exhibitions); Tube: Mile End.

Ragged School Museum E3

www.raggedschoolmuseum.org.uk

46-50 Copperfield Rd   (020) 8980 6405   1–2D

This museum of the history of the East End is housed in a Victorian canalside warehouse which, from 1895, formed part of the largest ragged (free) school in London. Appropriately, education and the life and work of Dr Barnardo are given particular emphasis, and there is a recreated Victorian classroom (which is used by school groups for re-enacted Victorian lessons). On the first Sun of the month there are family arts and crafts workshops. During the school holidays, activities are organised, from making Victorian sweets to treasure hunts. All are popular and space is limited. / Times: Wed and Thu 9am-5pm, 1st Sun of month 2pm-5pm; Tube: Mile End; Café.

Royal London Hospital Archives & Museum E1
www.bartsandthelondon.nhs.uk
St Augustine with St Philip's Church, Newark St
(020) 7377 7608   1–2D
The permanent exhibition about the history of the famous hospital is housed in the basement of a c19 church. Highlights include a small Hogarth drawing, George Washington's false teeth, nursing uniforms from the 1900s, documents relating to Elephant Man Joseph Merrick (and his hat) and a bust of WWI heroine Edith Cavell (who trained here), as well as her last letters from her condemned cell and the flag that covered her coffin. There are also videos, including films from the 1930s showing what it was like being a nurse and a patient then. / Times: Mon-Fri 10am-4.30pm (occasionally closed 1pm-2pm); Tube: Whitechapel; Picnic area.

Spitalfields Market E1
www.spitalfields.co.uk
Brushfield St   (020) 7247 8556   5–2D
The City's former fruit and vegetable market (vacated in 1991) has been transformed into a mixed development that is a particularly popular Sun destination. At the heart of the market are stalls selling arts and crafts, bric-à-brac, the latest fashions and organic food. Spitalfields makes a great lunch stop as, in summer, there is an International Food Village, (with offerings from Mexican chilli to Turkish kebabs). Regular special events include an alternative fashion week, a dog show, a community festival and a harvest festival. / Times: Mon-Wed, Fri 10am-6pm, Thu 7.30am-6pm, Sun 10am-5.30pm; Tube: Liverpool Street.

Thames Police Museum E1
www.thamespolicemuseum.org.uk
Marine Support Unit, 98 Wapping High St
(020) 7275 4421   1–3D
This collection documents the history of the Marine Police; artefacts date all the way back to 1798 – the date of the first organised London police force. Weapons, including cutlasses, model boats and uniforms, are all displayed in a pleasant setting overlooking the Thames. / Times: by written appt (groups and clubs preferred); Tube: Wapping.

Thurrock Museum
www.thurrock.gov.uk
Thameside Complex, Orsett Rd, Grays   (01375) 385484
A permanent gallery of the history of the Thurrock area, displaying archaeology from the Stone Age to the medieval period. There are also regularly changing temporary exhibitions based on local themes. / Times: Tue, Thu, Sat 9am-7pm, Mon, Wed, Fri 9am-5pm; BR: Grays.

Upminster Tithe Barn, Agricultural & Folk Museum

www.upminster.com

Hall Ln, Upminster   (07855) 633917

The barn is a large thatched, timber-framed structure, probably built around 1420. It contains a collection illustrating the farming, urban and social history of the community and shows the transition of the area from countryside to suburbia. There are over 13,000 exhibits, including old agricultural implements, farriers' tools, dairying equipment, bicycles, photographs, laundry paraphernalia (from the time when it was all done manually) and toys and games. / Times: 1st full weekend of month Apr-Oct, 2pm-6pm; BR: Upminster (then 248 bus); (light refreshment stand).

Upminster Windmill

www.upminsterwindmill.co.uk

St Mary's Ln, Upminster   (01708) 505865

This white five-storey mill was built in the early c19 and worked commercially until around 1935. It is owned by the London Borough of Havering and staffed by members of Hornchurch and District Historical Society. / Times: Apr-Sep, 3rd Sat and Sun of month, 2pm-5.30pm (also Open House Weekend and National Mills Weekend); BR: Upminster Station; Tube: Upminster.

V&A Museum of Childhood E2

www.vam.ac.uk/moc

Cambridge Heath Rd   (020) 8983 5200   1–2D

Housing the V&A's collection of toys, games, puppets, dolls and dolls houses (of which there are over 40), this repository of children's memorabilia offers quite enough to interest children and parents. There are free workshops for children on most Sat and Sun, and school holiday activities. The museum has an excellent supply of free literature about London attractions, particularly those in the East End. / Times: 10am-5.45pm daily; Tube: Bethnal Green; Café.

Vestry House Museum E17

www.walthamforest.gov.uk

Vestry Rd, Walthamstow   (020) 8509 1917

This prettily-situated workhouse (1730) was converted into a museum of local history in the 1930s. It is in the old village of Walthamstow (which is worth a visit in its own right). The most singular exhibit is probably the Bremer Car, which is claimed to be one of the first petrol-driven cars to be made in London. An original police cell (used between 1840 and 1870) is another curiosity. There is a programme of temporary exhibitions. / Times: Wed-Sun 10am-5pm; Tube: Walthamstow Central.

Waltham Abbey Church

www.walthamabbeychurch.co.uk

Highbridge St, Waltham Abbey   (01992) 767897

King Harold is said to be buried in the grounds of this Norman church, which was built in 1120 on the site of three previous churches. It was re-founded as an Augustinian abbey in 1177 by Henry II as part of his penance for the murder of Thomas Becket. The abbey was dissolved and partly destroyed in 1540 (the last in England to be closed by Henry VIII), leaving only the nave. The crypt centre contains shows an exhibition about the history of the town and abbey, which is close to Lee Valley Park (see also). / Times: 10am (noon on Sun and 11am on Wed)-6pm (4pm in winter); BR: Waltham Cross.

Whitechapel Art Gallery E1
www.whitechapel.org
80 Whitechapel High St
(020) 7522 7888, recorded information
(020) 7522 7878   5–2D
A major re-opening of spring 2009, this important non-commercial venue makes up for the absence of a permanent collection by holding an interesting series of temporary exhibitions. It occupies an atmospheric art nouveau building.
/ Times: Tue-Sun 11am-6pm (Thu 9pm); Tube: Aldgate East; Café.

William Morris Gallery E17
www.lbwf.gov.uk/wmg
Lloyd Park, Forest Rd   (020) 8527 3782
William Morris, born in Walthamstow in 1834, was probably the most influential designer and craftsman London has ever produced. He died in 1896, but his ideas were carried on by the Arts and Crafts movement into the 1920s, and many of his designs, especially for wallpaper and fabric, are still in production today. This delightful c18 house in its own grounds contains a display of Morris's work and personal memorabilia, together with examples of the products of his associates, Burne-Jones, Rossetti and Philip Webb. / Times: Thu-Sun 10am-5pm Tue-Wed pre-booked groups only; Tube: Walthamstow Central; Picnic area.

Outdoor attractions

Billingsgate Market E14
www.billingsgate-market.org.uk
Trafalgar Way, Isle of Dogs   (020) 7987 1118   1–3D
Though the name is an historic one, these days you have to journey to a decidedly modern structure on the Isle of Dogs to mingle with the merchants and buyers at the UK's largest inland fish market (with some 100 stalls). It sells on average 25,000 tonnes of fish and fish products every year. (The original building on Lower Thames Street – built in 1873 on a site that had been a market for centuries – still stands, but is used for offices nowadays. / Times: Tue-Sat 5am-8.30am, Sun (shellfish only) 6am-8am; DLR: Poplar.

Brick Lane Market E1
1–2D
Forget the papers – roll up early in the morning to start off Sun with a truly East End 'pile it high, sell it cheap' experience. 'It' might be almost anything. / Times: Sun 8am-2pm; Tube: Aldgate, Aldgate East, Liverpool Street, Shoreditch; Café.

Canary Wharf
www.canarywharf.com
(020) 7418 2783 (box office/events information)   1–3D
*Cesar Pelli's great tower (244m high) on the Isle of Dogs is, at
50 storeys, the tallest building in Britain. You don't need to
approach it to appreciate it – you can see it from all over
London – but if you do, there's an impressive shopping mall at
its base. There are many other shiny, new buildings around the
tower's base, which are worth a view – over 5 million square
feet of office and retail space has been created and occupied in
the area since 1991. The public spaces are well-kept and
provide many different views of the tower: look for the fountain
in Cabot Square, which is controlled by a computer that
changes the water level if it's windy to stop people getting
sprayed. There is a regular programme of arts and events,
many of which are free, including outside events in the
summer.* / Tube: Canary Wharf (DLR); Café, Restaurant.

Claybury Woods
www.redbridge.gov.uk
(020) 8501 1426
*Recently opened to the public, Claybury Woods cover almost
70 hectares of land and are comprised of two historic
woodlands – Claybury Wood and Hospital Hill Wood. Mainly
an oak/hornbeam woodland, the park also features a wide
variety of plant and animal life. Also available is a horse-riding
track, four ponds and two new wetlands. A signposted walk
around the park will take approximately three hours. Call for
an information leaflet.* / Times: 24 hours; Tube: Fairlop Central Line is the
closest tube station, catch the 275 at Barkingside towards Walthamstow and
get off on stop opposite Wannock Gardens, or catch the 169 from Barkingside
towards Clayhall for road entrances along the Fullwell Avenue.

Columbia Road Flower Market E2
www.columbia-flower-market.freewebspace.com
Columbia Rd   5–1D
*Every Sun morning this east London street (with a few
neighbouring alleys) bursts into bloom – you'll know you are
near the market when you see the occasional palm tree
walking down the street, possibly in the company of shrubs and
boxes of herbs. It's best to arrive early – it all gets terribly
crowded. A trip here combines well with a visit to Spitalfields
Market and Brick Lane.* / Times: Sun 8am-2pm; Tube: Old Street,
Liverpool Street, Shoreditch.

East Ham Nature Reserve E6
www.newham.gov.uk
Norman Rd   (020) 8470 4525
*The two suburban nature trails here have the mission of
introducing everyone to the joys of nature. Set in London's
largest churchyard (in use since Norman times, though the
oldest stones date from the c17), the trails are fully accessible
(including to people in wheelchairs). Ring to ensure the reserve
is open before you set off.* / Times: Tue-Fri 10am-5pm; Tube: East Ham.

Epping Forest
www.cityoflondon.gov.uk
(020) 8508 0028
*Two miles by 12, this ancient forest on the eastern fringe of
London (owned by the Corporation of London since Victorian
times) is the largest public open space in Essex. Great effort is
put into maintaining the landscape, with its diverse natural
history, and the area is designated as a Site of Special Scientific
Interest. Although the forest is a very popular destination, it's
big enough that you can lose yourself in it – real countryside
AND accessible from a tube station! A particular attraction is
Queen Elizabeth's Hunting Lodge (small charge to visit), near
Chingford, which is the only surviving Tudor 'hunt-standing'
(from which the monarch could view the hunt's progress). The
information centre at High Beech organises occasional walks
through the forest (details from the number given). At this spot
(it's around two miles from Loughton), there is an easy-access
path and also tracks that are popular with horse riders and
mountain bikers.* / Times: visitor centre summer 11am-6pm, winter
10am-3pm; Tube: Epping, Theydon Bois, Loughton, Snaresbrook, Debden.

Flitch Way
www.essexcc.gov.uk
Rayne Station Centre, Station Rd, Rayne   (01376) 340262
*The Flitch Way is a country park passing through 15 miles of
countryside along the former Bishop's Stortford to Braintree
railway line. Your journey passes wildlife-rich railway cuttings,
Victorian stations, farmland, villages and woodland. The Centre
has an exhibition room of local history, open on Sun.*
/ Times: 8am-dusk; BR: Braintree; Picnic area.

Greenway
www.newham.gov.uk
(020) 8472 1430 (ask for Park & Leisure Services)
*Formerly less romantically described as the Northern Outfall
Sewer Embankment, this elevated feature of the landscape was
built in the 1860s to provide a sewage and drainage system for
east London. Shedding its original image, the four mile long
path now has been developed as a wildlife habitat and provides
unfettered open spaces for walkers and cyclists. The route
begins from Royal Dock Road in E6, and runs to Stratford High
Road in E15 and beyond into Hackney. Along the entire route,
there are access points for visitors and noticeboards about
native flora and fauna.* / Times: 6am-dusk; Tube: Beckton (DLR), West
Ham; Café, Restaurant, Picnic area.

Greenwich Foot Tunnel E14
www.greenwich.gov.uk
(020) 8854 8888 ext 5493 (to confirm lift times)   1–3D
*The tunnel, opened in 1902, connects Greenwich with the Isle
of Dogs and was built because the steamboat ferry was
contributing to excessive congestion of the river at this point. It
lies 10 metres below the low water mark, is 390m long and is
made of cast iron segments, lined with concrete and tiled. New*

lifts were installed in 1992, replacing equipment which had lasted since 1904. After 1999, when the Jubilee Line opened between Greenwich and Canary Wharf, the practical function of the tunnel was somewhat overshadowed, although the appeal of walking under the Thames continues to attract children of all ages. / Times: lift service, Mon-Sat 7am-7pm, Sun 10am-5.30pm; tunnel 24 hours; Tube: Greenwich, Island Gardens (DLR).

Hackney City Farm E2
www.hackneycityfarm.co.uk
1a Goldsmith's Row   (020) 7729 6381   1–2D
Hackney City Farm keeps as full a range as possible of traditional farm livestock in its one and a half-acre site. In spring, the lambs and calves are a particular reason to take the children. Feeding takes place around 4pm daily. / Times: Tue-Sun 10am-4.30pm (and bank hols); Tube: Bethnal Green; BR: Hackney; Café.

Hainault Forest Country Park
www.hainaultforest.co.uk
(020) 8500 7353
This square mile of woodland was dedicated to the public in 1906 and is one of the few remaining vestiges of the great forest of Essex and Waltham (see also Epping Forest). It is a Site of Special Scientific Interest because of the ancient woodland, pollarded trees and flora and fauna. Foxburrows Farm conserves rare breeds and employs traditional farm practices. Activities in the summer events programme might include a storytelling picnic, a fungi-finding expedition, orienteering and a bat search. In the winter, there are bird-feeding days and Christmas decorations workshops. There is a brochure of events which can be obtained by calling the above number. / Times: 7am-dusk; Tube: Hainault then 247 or 362 bus (or BR to Romford or Ilford then 150 or 247 bus); Café.

Hainault Lodge Nature Reserve
www.hainaultforest.co.uk
(020) 8501 1426
Redbridge Borough's first Local Nature Reserve is remarkable for its views across London and for the variety of habitats within its small area. You need to obtain permission and arrange an appointment (from Nature Conservation Ranger Team, tel 020 8599 7818 or John Carter on 01708 720325) to enter the 14-acre site (adjacent to the park), but everyone is welcome and tours can be arranged. Creatures you might see include many nesting birds and small mammals – if you are very lucky you might spot the rare Black Rabbit. / Tube: Hainault then 247 or 362 bus (or BR to Romford or Ilford then 150 or 247 bus).

Hatfield Forest
www.nationaltrust.org.uk
Estate Office, Takeley, Bishop's Stortford   (01279) 870678
This rare surviving example of a medieval royal hunting forest is a Site of Special Scientific Interest and a national nature reserve. The forest comprises over 400 hectares of ancient coppice woodland with two ornamental lakes, the c18 Shell House, a stream and a marsh reserve. / Times: dawn-dusk; BR: Bishop's Stortford; Café, Picnic area.

Lee Valley Regional Park, Essex
www.leevalleypark.org.uk
Lee Valley Park Information Centre, Abbey Gardens,
Waltham Abbey, Essex EN9 1XQ   (01992) 702200
*Since 1967, the derelict valley of the River Lee has been being
transformed into over 1,000 acres of 'green chain', extending
out from Hackney, via Tottenham and Enfield, to the more truly
rural delights of Hertfordshire and Essex. You can walk the
whole 23 miles on the towpath, or cycle it – it is part of the
National Cycle Network linking Hertfordshire with Harwich.
Natural attractions include a variety of bird life and a dragonfly
sanctuary. Man-made items of interest include some pretty and
historic c18 buildings, among them the largest restored tidal
mill left standing in Britain (open Sun, 2pm-4pm, small charge,
(020) 8215 0050) and the Clock Mill. Within the park, you
can also find Lee Valley Walk, a 50-mile regional walking trail
from London to Luton, and River Lee Country Park, where you
might be lucky enough to spot the rare bittern or smew (bird
hides are open to all on weekends). If you're planning a visit,
contact the Countryside Centre to pick up relevant leaflets. All
parts of the Park are easily accessible from the rail line which
runs alongside. / Times: Mon-Fri 9am-5pm, Sat and Sun 9am-5pm (closed
for lunch between 1pm-2pm); Tube: Tottenham Hale; Picnic area.*

Mudchute Park & Farm E14
www.mudchute.org
Pier St   (020) 7515 5901   1–3D
*The largest urban farm in London, this 32-acre site is the most
significant open space on the Isle of Dogs. It includes a riding
arena, fields, a wild section, a picnic area and woodlands.
Because it's several times bigger than most of the other farms
– complete with its own grassland for grazing – it can be run
largely as if it were a small farm in the country. On the
livestock front, the speciality here is sheep, of which a wide
variety are kept, but there are also cattle, goats and pigs. Each
year there is a family day in July. / Times: summer 9am-5pm, winter
10am-4.30pm; Tube: Crossharbour (DLR), Mudchute (DLR); Café.*

Newham City Farm E6
www.newham.gov.uk
Stansfeld Rd, Beckton   (020) 7474 4960   1–2D
*This four and a half-acre farm has a wide range of livestock,
including a shire horse, a donkey, cows, pigs, sheep, goats,
chickens, ducks and geese. It is well geared up for casual
visitors – 50,000 people pass through the gates each year.
/ Times: summer Tue-Sun 10am-5pm, winter Tue-Sun 10am-4pm; Tube: Royal
Albert (DLR), or Plaistow (then 262 bus); Café, Picnic area.*

Petticoat Lane E1
*Certainly the best-known market in the East End, and possibly
in London. The Sun morning activity here is a phenomenon
worth seeing whether or not you have any desire to invest in
some of the low-cost clothes which are the market's speciality.
/ Times: Mon-Fri 10am-2.30pm Sun 9am-2pm; Tube: Liverpool Street, Aldgate.*

Spitalfields City Farm E1

www.spitalfieldscityfarm.org
Pedley St   (020) 7247 8762   1–2D
Despite its small size (one and a half-acres) and location (on former wasteground), this popular attraction manages to squeeze in most of the usual farm animals. Look out also for special events at Christmas and Easter, and during the summer, some of which are free. In addition, community members can take the National Proficiency Test Council Course (NPTC) in horticulture training for free. It begins in the spring and runs through autumn, averaging about 90 hours of training. / Times: Tue-Sun 10am-4pm; Tube: Aldgate East, Shoreditch.

St Katharine Docks E1

www.skdocks.co.uk
1–3D
St Katharine's by the Tower (as the area is more properly called) is a fine collection of buildings, principally designed by the great c19 engineer Thomas Telford, restored to make a very attractive marina. It offers by far the nicest place for a riverside stroll in central London – the Tower of London and Tower Bridge provide a dramatic backdrop. In the summer, there is lunchtime music several times a week. / Tube: Tower Hill; Café.

Stepping Stones Farm E1

www.aboutbritain.com/steppingstonesfarm.htm
Stepney Way   (020) 7790 8204   1–2D
This eight-acre farm has all the main types of farm animals – cows, pigs, donkeys, sheep, goats, chickens, ducks and geese, as well as rabbits, guinea pigs and ferrets. There is also a picnic garden and play area. The venture is run entirely by volunteers and trainees, and partly funded by the sale of produce and home produce. Look out for events during school holidays (such as the Easter egg hunt), some of which are free. / Times: Tue-Sun 10am-4pm; Tube: Stepney Green, Limehouse (DLR); Café.

Thames Barrier Park E16

www.thamesbarrierpark.org.uk
North Woolwich Rd   (020) 7476 3741
London's first new urban park for 70 years is rather a remarkable sight and has won a bevy of awards since its opening in 2000. Features include a 3km trench, 5m deep, to provide a microclimate for plants, and a riverside promenade. / Times: dawn-dusk; Tube: Silver Town (DLR).

Thorndon Country Park & Hartswood

www.essexcc.gov.uk
(01277) 211250 (Essex Ranger Service)
A medley of parks, lakes, woods and golf clubs makes up this rural retreat, and there's lots of history and nature to wander through, including a deer park little changed since the c16. / Times: park 8am-dusk; Countryside Centre 10am-5pm (winter until dusk); BR: Brentwood (then 151 bus to Halfway House or 73 bus to Warley).

Tower Hamlets Cemetery Park E3
www.towerhamletscemetery.org
Southern Gr   (07904) 186 981   1–2D
Built as a model necropolis for wealthy Londoners in 1841, this 27-acre site was used for burials up until 1966. A period of neglect followed, during which the local flora and fauna established themselves with a vengeance – in 1986, Tower Hamlets decided to make a virtue of necessity and declared the place a nature reserve, now boasting 20 species of butterfly and some 35 types of bird. Some very fine Victorian tombs remain, and there is also a tree trail, which takes about 45 minutes to complete. Tue is generally 'drop-in' volunteer day, but call ahead to check first. / Times: 8am-dusk; Tube: Mile End.

Victoria Park E3
www.victoria-park-lakes.co.uk
Old Ford Rd   (020) 8985 1957   1–2D
In the 1840s, concern grew in east London about the lack of any recreational space for the burgeoning population. Fearing unrest, the government sold York House in Westminster to pay for the establishment of the new Victoria Park (of 220 acres) to be a 'Green Lung' for the area. It is still the only large, formal park in the East End. Its style is very much in keeping with its name – it has lakes and fountains, one of which is a Gothic drinking fountain from 1861, large areas of bedding plants, a children's playground, a bandstand (with live music on Sun afternoons in July and August) and a herd of fallow deer. Recent years have seen much refurbishment of the facilities. The oldest model boat club in the world meets here most Sun mornings during the summer. / Times: 7.30am-dusk; Tube: Bethnal Green, Mile End.

Walthamstow Market E17
www.walthamforest.gov.uk
Walthamstow High St   (020) 8496 3000   1–1D
Claiming to be the longest street market in Europe, this mile-long stretch of stalls sells a plethora of wares from antiques to designer clothes. Sun lunchtimes see a farmers' market. / Times: Tue-Sun 8am-5pm; Tube,BR: Walthamstow Central.

West Ham Park E7
www.cityoflondon.gov.uk
Upton Ln   (020) 8472 3584
This 77-acre park in West Ham has been owned and run by the Corporation of London since 1874. The recreational facilities include a large children's playground, tennis courts and a seven-acre formal garden in the south east corner of the park. During the summer, there are children's entertainers at the bandstand, and Sun afternoon concerts. / Times: 7.30am-30 mins before dusk; Tube: Plaistow, Stratford; Picnic area.

Maps

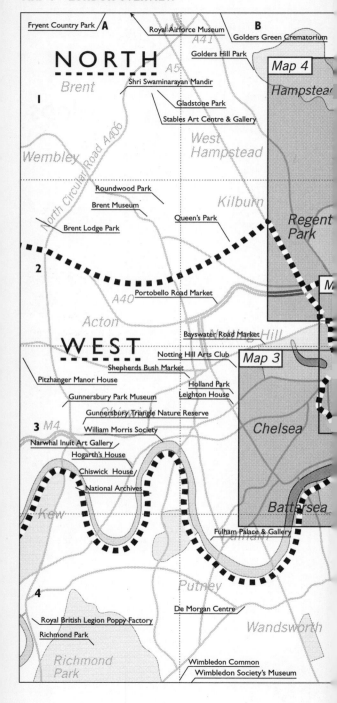

MAP I – LONDON OVERVIEW

A
B

Fryent Country Park

Royal Airforce Museum

Golders Green Crematorium

Golders Hill Park

Map 4

NORTH

Hampstead

Brent

Shri Swaminarayan Mandir

I

Gladstone Park

*West
Hampstead*

Stables Art Centre & Gallery

Wembley

North Circular Road A406

Roundwood Park

Kilburn

Brent Museum

Queen's Park

*Regent
Park*

Brent Lodge Park

2

A40

Portobello Road Market

Acton

Hill

M

WEST

Bayswater Road Market

Notting Hill Arts Club

Map 3

Shepherds Bush Market

Pitzhanger Manor House

Holland Park

Gunnersbury Park Museum

Leighton House

Gunnersbury Triangle Nature Reserve

3 M4

William Morris Society

Chelsea

Narwhal Inuit Art Gallery

Hogarth's House

Chiswick House

National Archives

Kew

Battersea

Fulham Palace & Gallery

4

De Morgan Centre

Royal British Legion Poppy Factory

Wandsworth

Richmond Park

Putney

*Richmond
Park*

Wimbledon Common

Wimbledon Society's Museum

MAP I – LONDON OVERVIEW

Waterlow Park
Lauderdale House Community Arts Centre
Railway Fields Local Nature Reserve
Abney Park Cemetery
Walthamstow Market

C
D

Highgate

Stoke Newington

Hackney Marshes

M102

Clowns International Archives
Hackney Museum

Dalston

Geffrye Museum

Camden

Victoria Park

Islington

Hackney City Farm
Chisenhale Gallery
V&A Museum of Childhood
Newham City Farm

EAST

Tower Hamlets Cemetery
Ragged School Museum
Spitalfields City Farm
Matt's Gallery
Stepney Stepping Stones Farm
Royal London Hospital Archives
Brick Lane Market
St Katharine's Dock
Billingsgate Market
Thames Police Museum

2

Map 5

C E N T R A L

City

Canary Wharf

Pumphouse Museum
Surrey Docks Farm
Island History Trust
Bermondsey Antiques Market
Cuming Museum
Mudchute Park & Farm

Southwark

Isle of Dogs

A3

Beaconsfield Contemporary Art
Vauxhall City Farm
Greenwich Foot Tunnel
Greenwich Markets
Old Royal Naval College
Chumleigh Gardens
New Covent Garden Market
Greenwich Park
Old Royal Observatory
Brooking Collection
Greenwich Heritage Centre
Blackheath
Age Exchange Reminiscence Centre

Camberwell

Greenwich

South London Art Gallery

Nunhead Cemetery

Lewisham

Brixton

Clapham

SOUTH

Brixton Market
Photofusion

London Wildlife Centre

Dulwich

Dulwich Park

Sydenham Hill Wood Local Nature Preserve
Horniman Museum

Belair Park

MAP 2 – CENTRAL LONDON

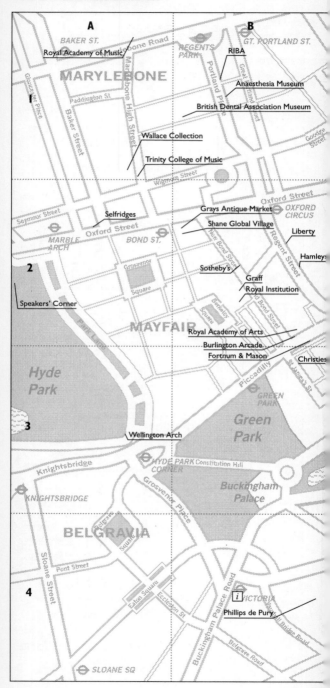

MAP 2 – CENTRAL LONDON

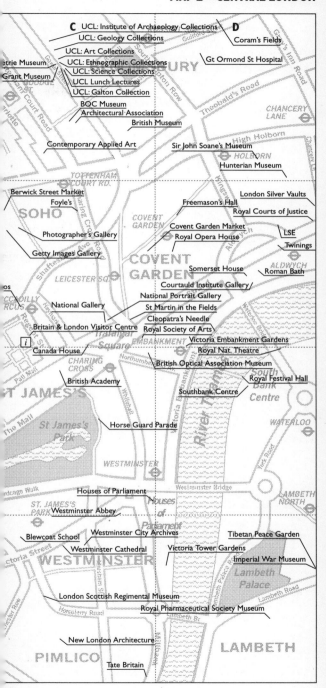

C UCL: Institute of Archaeology Collections **D**
UCL: Geology Collections
Coram's Fields
UCL: Art Collections
Gt Ormond St Hospital
UCL: Ethnographic Collections
tetrie Museum
UCL: Science Collections
Grant Museum
UCL: Lunch Lectures
UCL: Galton Collection
CHANCERY
LANE
BOC Museum
Architectural Association
British Museum

Contemporary Applied Art
Sir John Soane's Museum
High Holborn
HOLBORN
Hunterian Museum

TOTTENHAM
COURT RD.
Berwick Street Market
London Silver Vaults
Foyle's
Freemason's Hall
Royal Courts of Justice
SOHO
COVENT
GARDEN
Covent Garden Market
Photographer's Gallery
Royal Opera House
LSE
Getty Images Gallery
Twinings
COVENT
ALDWYCH
LEICESTER SQ.
GARDEN
Somerset House
Roman Bath
Courtauld Institute Gallery
os
National Portrait Gallery
CCADILLY
National Gallery
St Martin in the Fields
RCUS
Cleopatra's Needle
Britain & London Visitor Centre
Royal Society of Arts
i
EMBANKMENT
Victoria Embankment Gardens
Canada House
Royal Nat. Theatre
CHARING
CROSS
British Optical Association Museum
South
ST JAMES'S
Bank
British Academy
Royal Festival Hall
Southbank Centre
Centre
WATERLOO
Horse Guard Parade
The Mall
St James's
Park
WESTMINSTER

Houses of Parliament
Westminster Bridge
LAMBETH
NORTH
Houses of
ST. JAMES'S
PARK
Westminster Abbey
rbridge Walk
of
Westminster City Archives
Blewcoat School
Tibetan Peace Garden
Parliament
Westminster Cathedral
Victoria Tower Gardens
Imperial War Museum
WESTMINSTER
Lambeth
Palace
London Scottish Regimental Museum
Royal Pharmaceutical Society Museum

New London Architecture
LAMBETH
PIMLICO
Tate Britain

MAP 3 – WEST LONDON (SW POSTCODES)

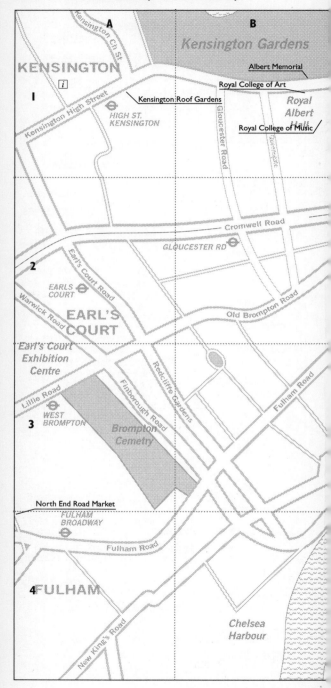

A   **B**

Kensington Ch St.

Kensington Gardens

KENSINGTON

Albert Memorial

Royal College of Art

i

Kensington Roof Gardens

1

Kensington High Street

Royal Albert Hall

HIGH ST. KENSINGTON

Gloucester Road

Royal College of Music

Queensgate

Cromwell Road

GLOUCESTER RD.

Earl's Court Road

2

EARLS COURT

Warwick Road

EARL'S COURT

Old Brompton Road

Earl's Court Exhibition Centre

Redcliffe Gardens

Fulham Road

Lillie Road

Finborough Road

WEST BROMPTON

3

Brompton Cemetery

North End Road Market

FULHAM BROADWAY

Fulham Road

4 FULHAM

New King's Road

Chelsea Harbour

MAP 3 – WEST LONDON (SW POSTCODES)

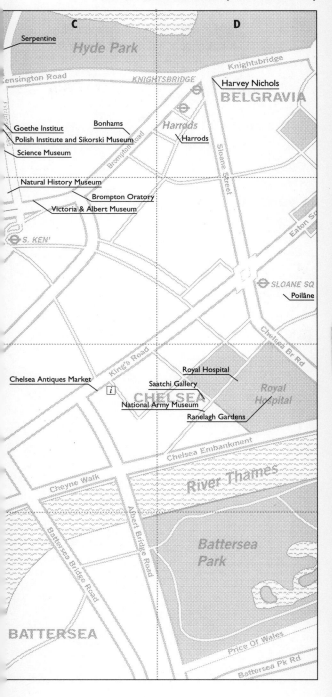

MAP 4 – NORTH LONDON

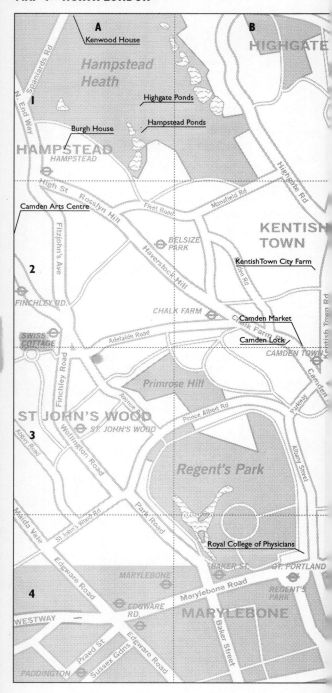

MAP 4 – NORTH LONGON

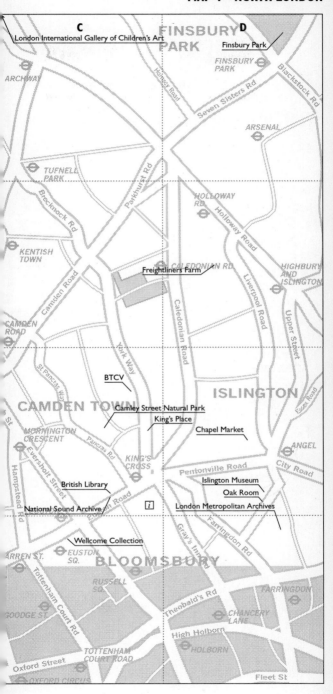

C

London International Gallery of Children's Art

FINSBURY PARK

Finsbury Park

FINSBURY PARK

D

ARCHWAY

Horsey Road

Blackstock Rd

Seven Sisters Rd

ARSENAL

TUFNELL PARK

Parkhurst Rd

Brecknock Rd

HOLLOWAY RD

Holloway Road

KENTISH TOWN

Camden Road

CALEDONIAN RD

Freightliners Farm

HIGHBURY AND ISLINGTON

Caledonian Road

Liverpool Road

Upper Street

CAMDEN ROAD

York Way

St Pancras Way

BTCV

ISLINGTON

Essex Road

CAMDEN TOWN

Camley Street Natural Park

King's Place

Chapel Market

MORNINGTON CRESCENT

Pancras Rd

ANGEL

City Road

Eversholt Street

KING'S CROSS

Pentonville Road

Hampstead Rd

British Library

Islington Museum

Oak Room

National Sound Archive

London Metropolitan Archives

Gray's Inn Rd

Farringdon Rd

Wellcome Collection

WARREN ST.

EUSTON SQ.

BLOOMSBURY

FARRINGDON

Tottenham Court Rd

RUSSELL SQ.

Theobald's Rd

CHANCERY LANE

GOODGE ST.

High Holborn

Oxford Street

TOTTENHAM COURT ROAD

HOLBORN

OXFORD CIRCUS

Fleet St

MAP 5 – THE CITY

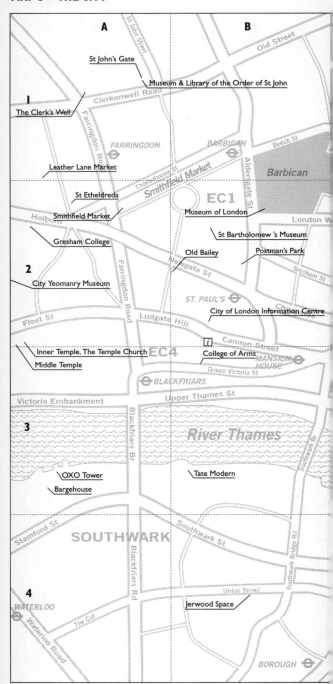

A **B**

St John's Gate

Museum & Library of the Order of St John

I Clerkenwell Road

The Clerk's Well

FARRINGDON BARBICAN Beech St.

Barbican

Leather Lane Market

Smithfield Market

St Etheldreda EC1

Smithfield Market Museum of London London W

Holborn

Gresham College St Bartholomew's Museum

Old Bailey Postman's Park

Gresham St.

2 Newgate St.

City Yeomanry Museum

ST. PAUL'S

Farringdon Road City of London Information Centre

Fleet St. Ludgate Hill

Cannon Street

Inner Temple, The Temple Church EC4 College of Arms MANSION

Middle Temple HOUSE

Queen Victoria St.

BLACKFRIARS

Victoria Embankment Upper Thames St.

3 River Thames

Blackfriars Br. Southwark Br.

OXO Tower Tate Modern

Bargehouse

Stamford St. SOUTHWARK Southwark St.

Blackfriars Rd. Southwark Bridge Rd.

4 Union Street

WATERLOO Jerwood Space

The Cut

Waterloo Road

BOROUGH

MAP 5 – THE CITY

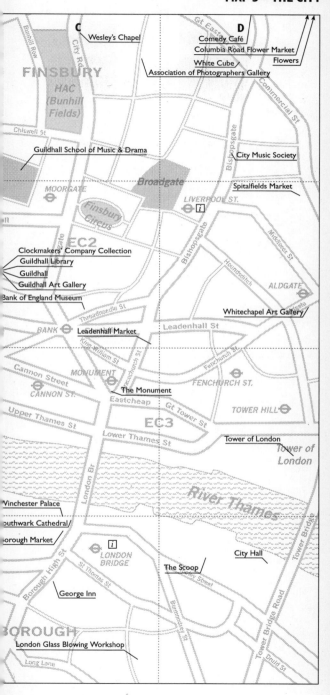

C

Wesley's Chapel

D

Comedy Café

Columbia Road Flower Market

Flowers

White Cube

Association of Photographers Gallery

FINSBURY

HAC
(Bunhill
Fields)

Chiswell St

Commercial St

Guildhall School of Music & Drama

City Music Society

Bishopsgate

Broadgate

Spitalfields Market

MOORGATE

Finsbury
Circus

LIVERPOOL ST.

i

Middlesex St

EC2

Clockmakers' Company Collection

Guildhall Library

Guildhall

Guildhall Art Gallery

Bank of England Museum

Bishopsgate

Houndsditch

ALDGATE

Whitechapel Art Gallery

Threadneedle St

BANK

Leadenhall Market

Leadenhall St

King William St

Fenchurch St

MONUMENT

The Monument

Cannon Street

CANNON ST.

Eastcheap

Gt Tower St

FENCHURCH ST.

TOWER HILL

Upper Thames St

EC3

Lower Thames St

Tower of London

Tower of
London

London Br

River Thames

Winchester Palace

Southwark Cathedral

Borough Market

i

LONDON
BRIDGE

St Thomas St

Tower Bridge

Tower Bridge Road

City Hall

The Scoop

Borough High St

George Inn

Druid St

BOROUGH

London Glass Blowing Workshop

Long Lane

Indexes

Index by type of attraction

Index by type of attraction

Alphabetical index